T0210705

Digital Learning in Motion

Digital Learning in Motion provides a theoretical analysis of learning and related learning media in society. The book explores how changing media affects learning environments, which changes the learning itself, showing that learning is always in motion.

This book expounds upon the concept of learning, reconstructing how learning unfolds and analyzing the discourse around pedagogy and Bildung in the age of new digital media. It further discusses in detail the threefold relationship between learning and motion, considering how learning is based on motion, generated by new experiences and changes with the environment and through its own mediatization. The book presents a normative model that outlines how learning can be structured on the basis of society's values and self-understanding discourses in the digital age.

This book will be of great interest for academics, postgraduate students, and researchers in the fields of digital learning and inclusion, education research, educational theory, communication and cultural studies.

David Kergel is a Professor (Tenure) at the IUBH University for Applied Sciences and Co-editor of the book series 'Perspectives on Education in the Digital Age' (Routledge). His research interests include qualitative educational research, media education, and diversity in the digital age.

Perspectives on Education in the Digital Age
Series Editors: David Kergel and Birte Heidkamp

The process of digitalization is leading to a fundamental social change affecting all spheres of social life. In the pedagogical field there is a need for re-structuring key concepts such as learning, teaching and education that considers socio-economic and cultural changes.

Perspectives on Education in the Digital Age explores the process of coming to terms with socio-economic and socio-cultural shifts arising from digitalization and discusses this process with reference to its effects on education. The Series provides a forum for discussion of critical, integrative analyses of social transformations in the digital age, drawn from different fields such as the humanities, social sciences and economics. The aim of the Series is to analyse the implications of cultural change on education in the digital age by bringing together interdisciplinary dialogue and different theoretical approaches.

Epistemological Approaches to Digital Learning in Educational Contexts
Edited by Linda Daniela

New Perspectives on Virtual and Augmented Reality
Finding New Ways to Teach in a Transformed
Learning Environment
Edited by Linda Daniela

Digital Learning in Motion
From Book Culture to the Digital Age
David Kergel

For more information about this series, please visit: https://www.routledge.com

Digital Learning in Motion

From Book Culture to the Digital Age

David Kergel

Routledge
Taylor & Francis Group

LONDON AND NEW YORK

First published 2021
by Routledge
2 Park Square, Milton Park, Abingdon, Oxon OX14 4RN

and by Routledge
52 Vanderbilt Avenue, New York, NY 10017

Routledge is an imprint of the Taylor & Francis Group, an informa business

British Library Cataloguing-in-Publication Data
A catalogue record for this book is available from the British Library

Library of Congress Cataloging-in-Publication Data
A catalog record has been requested for this book

ISBN: 978-1-138-36674-9 (hbk)
ISBN: 978-0-429-43014-5 (ebk)

Typeset in Bembo
by codeMantra

Contents

Figures

Table

Chapter 1

Introduction

At a first glance, learning seems to be an anthropological constant: The human being is a 'deficient being'; in order to survive the human being needs to acquire knowledge about the world. The process through which the human being acquires knowledge about the world can be termed 'learning.' Learning can be defined as a constant and sustainable change in behavior or behavioral potential of an individual (Winkel, Petermann & Petermann, 2006). From this point of view learning can be analyzed without any socio-historical contextualization.

The concept of learning is an open concept. This openness can be considered a strength since a conceptual examination of learning sharpens the analytical perception of the phenomenon 'learning.' Despite the different definitional approaches, experience can be identified as the basis of learning.

Experience is a key concept for the discussion about the definition of the notion learning. The term 'experience' shows that learning is based on impressions, contents, information, and thus on the environment. Learning is an effect of processing environmental perception and interaction. As a process, learning is bound to experiences. Experiences are made in an active confrontation with the world. Where activity is, movement or motion exists. Learning has a threefold relationship with the term motion. On one hand, learning is based on motion. On the other hand, learning is expansive because new knowledge is generated by new experiences. At the same time, learning changes with the environment and with its own mediatization. The change of media changes the environment which learners deal with and, therefore, changes the learning itself. Learning is, therefore, always in motion. The following considerations expound upon these aspects.

The main thesis assumes that the established discourse about learning and its subtextual understanding of the human being is a discursive effect of civil society. To unfold this thesis, it is important to distinguish between the anthropological constant and the discursive frame in which this anthropological constant is thematized. From a phenomenological point of view, it seems an ineluctable fact that the human being is a learning being. But the way we are aware of learning as a phenomenon depends on the socio-historical context in which we are embedded. For me, as a European researcher, the socio-historical is defined by civil society and its development.

This analysis methodically reconstructs how learning unfolds in civil society. It is based on the thesis that learning is always bound to the mediatization of society: With medial change learning processes also change. Genealogical reconstruction leads from the book culture of the Gutenberg Galaxy to the Electronic Age. Based on this reconstruction, a normative model will be proposed of how learning can be structured on the basis of bourgeois society's values and self-understanding discourses in the digital age. In order to develop such a proposal and to carry out a genealogical reconstruction of learning, it is necessary to confront concepts of education and upbringing. Bildung and Erziehung can be defined as pedagogical forms of care that have been developed in civil society. Bildung and Erziehung stand for different aspects of bourgeois self-transformation processes and each provides a different lens to interpret learning. Together, Bildung and Erziehung form a basic analytical heuristic for reconstructing the development of learning from book culture to the digital age.

This method of reconstruction is Eurocentric. The analysis focuses on the concept of learning, as it has been developed in civil European society. Bourgeois society is the objectual focus of this investigation, so the limits of this research are explicitly pointed out. Learning in bourgeois society becomes an object of knowledge that can then be compared with learning concepts from other cultures in following intercultural analyses.

1.1 The birth of learning from the spirit of civil society

Civil society can be defined as a secular idea of political and social order based on the rational competence of the citizen: The citizen is defined as an individual which is able to argue, act, and decide in a rational manner (cf. Kergel, 2013; Krämer-Badoni, 1978). The citizen is responsible for his actions himself.

This political idea is linked with a specific economic concept: Liberal market economy. This linkage is different from socialist-oriented concepts of society. Socialist-oriented concepts of society also assume the rational competence of individuals. However, socialist-oriented concepts of society define the question of ownership in contrast with the concept of ownership of civil society.

From an epistemological point of view, civil society is based on a voluntaristic-rational concept of the subject. Via voluntaristic-rational reflection strategies, the bourgeois subject constitutes herself independently of otherworldly instances. Because of this, the concept of reason implies also the concept of freedom. To reflect rationally about the world, the subject needs to be free to act according to his insight and to judge what exists on a rational basis. Thus, the epistemology of civil society is based on the premise that reason unfolds from the rational subjectivity of the human being: the individual must examine and judge everything by the force and power of her cognition. The concept of the self-determined individual as citizen of a civil society is a bourgeois concept that is delimited by the culture and the self-understanding discourses of feudalism. In the increasing establishment of bourgeois culture and civil society such delimitation concepts emerged in different societal fields. The constituting processes of civil society can be traced beyond the 19th century to the emancipation of the bourgeoisie. The rise of the bourgeoisie to the dominating class in Europe was accompanied by the cultural and political collapse of feudalism. To analyze the dominant culture's social transformation from feudalism to civil society and bourgeois culture, one can refer to the concept of symbolic order.

1.2 Symbolic order of civil society

Symbolic order is an analytical category which describes the symbolic dimension of power structures. The symbolic order is the structure of meaning of hierarchies and relations of dependence. It provides reasons and an ideology for the hierarchical structures of social spaces. The truth claims and codes of a symbolic order provide rules of conduct and therewith certainty through points of orientation – you know to behave. If you need to go to a restroom, you orientate yourself by the iconic representations on the restroom doors. As a man, you 'normally' choose the restroom at which door a male icon is affixed. You know where to go! As a woman you 'normally' choose the restroom at which door a female icon is affixed. You know where to go! At the same time you choose the appropriate door, you also acknowledge the binary gender structure which is part of most symbolic orders. The symbolic order constructs a meaningful space in which hierarchies and power structures are discursively legitimized and performatively reproduced. But the symbolic order also constitutes a space of resistance where meaning can be questioned. For example, a person who wants to protest against the binary gender structure can choose the 'inappropriate' restroom door or deface the doors' iconic gender representations as a form of resistance. Despite such acts of resistance and questioning of the symbolic order, the symbolic order represents the symbolic dimension of power structures.

With new power structures new symbolic orders are constructed. For example, coffee became the ideological beverage of civil society. In the era of absolutism, the French nobility drank hot chocolate. The sweet beverage represented pleasure. Coffee, with its activating effect, represents the activity of the citizen in a civil society. As the power of the citizen and civil society increased and the power of the nobility decreased, coffee achieved popularity (cf. Schivelbusch, 1990). With the civil society a new symbolic order emerged, which can be reconstructed through an analysis of the symbolical meaning of beverage (coffee instead of hot chocolate). On a cultural level, the process which led from feudalism to civil society and bourgeois culture is called the Enlightenment. The Enlightenment accompanied the rise of the bourgeoisie as a cultural transformation process. In other words, the Enlightenment can be interpreted as the cultural manifestation of the bourgeoisie and civil society. Throughout the course of the Enlightenment, critical arguments were placed against 'irrational' divine hierarchies and 'irrational' dependency relationships. Via rational thinking, the bourgeois subject differentiates itself from irrational hierarchies and dependencies of feudalism. Consequently, the bourgeois subject is rational based and therefore emancipative, since it differentiates himself critically and reflexively from irrational claims to power.

In the sense of a semiotic 'search for traces,' the erosion of the symbolic order of feudalism can be traced through the shift of cultural practices. For example, the erosion of feudalism manifests itself metonymically in the guillotining of Louis XVI (cf. Kergel, 2013). Blessed with the king's salvation, the French king symbolized the divine order of the sacred and absolutist royalty. In his speech "On the King's Fate" (27 December 1792), St Just urged to detach from the concept of nobility:

> Citizens, when first you deliberated the question of this trial, I told you that a king was outside the state, and by nature above the law. This is why whatever covenant may have been agreed upon between the People and the King (in this case an illegitimate covenant), it did not bind him.[1]
>
> (St Just, 1792, para. 2)

In the course of the French Revolution, Louis XVI also became the legal figure "Citizen Capet." Between absolutist royalty and bourgeois individual, Louis XVI/Citizen Capet represents two legal individuals in one person. With the execution of the person Louis XVI/Citizen Capet on January 21, 1793, two societal individuals were executed at the same time. The bourgeois rational-based secularization of society is semiotically underlined by the practice of guillotining; as an execution practice, guillotining is discursively thematized as a rational method of killing. During the French Revolution, all those who were sentenced to death were subjected to the guillotine. The guillotine rationalized the practice of state-sanctioned killing. Thus, the guillotine was distinct from execution practices that were part of semiotic penal culture of the Middle Ages. Before the introduction of the guillotine, the execution procedure represented the significance of crime and the status of the delinquent. Beheading, for example, was an honorable form of killing and was reserved for nobles. Hanging, in turn, had humiliating connotations.

The symbolic meaning of a rational killing is part of the bourgeois secularization process. This secularization process can be interpreted as cultural manifestation of the rise of the bourgeoisie and civil society. The penal system symbolically manifested bourgeois value systems: "Social values and retributive intuitions influence the symbolic meaning of punishment and this symbolic meaning in turn influences its social effects" (Hanna, 2008, S. 91). The semiotic change of the death penalty is embedded in discursive shifts and can be understood as part of the secularization process of the Enlightenment.

The establishment of the bourgeois culture affected all areas of society. Its basic dichotomy was the demarcation of the bourgeois from the 'leading culture' of the nobility. In its origins, bourgeois culture was narrated as counterculture. The discursive demarcation strategies towards the culture of nobility created a bourgeois space of thought and discourse. Out of this space of thought and discourse bourgeois culture successively emerged as the leading Western culture. As mentioned earlier, bourgeois counterculture and its basic dichotomy of nobility's irrational/alienated/decadent culture versus the bourgeoisie's rational culture emerged in almost every societal field.

One example is *Empfindsamkeit* (sentimentalism) as a concept of bourgeois emotionality. Here one can refer to the research results of Hansen. Hansen (1989) used a genealogically oriented approach to reconstruct the bourgeois discourses of emotion. In his research Hansen examined the difference between bourgeois discourses of self-understanding and a – discursively ascribed – culture of the nobility. The focus of his analysis is the bourgeois programmatics of Empfindsamkeit. Hansen describes the lasting effect of this emotional concept, which according to Hansen also defined our discursive framing of emotions:

> The most extensive, most differentiated emotional program that penetrates into all areas of culture, which we know, is the sensitivity of the 18th century. From this, the bourgeois culture of emotion developed, which to this day forms the manners of the middle classes.
> (Hansen, 1989, p. 39, translation David Kergel)

Empfindsamkeit represents a bourgeois redefinition of emotionality. The bourgeois topos of critical thinking was flanked by a 'sentimental' emotional discourse. Empfindsamkeit has origins in France and England at the beginning of the 1700s and particularly flourished in the pre-revolutionary period from 1740 to 1790. In Germany, the concept of Empfindsamkeit was coined by Lessing. Lessing suggested the adjective *empfindsam* (*Yoricks empfindsame Reise*, 1769) for the translation of Stern's novel *A Sentimental Journey Through France and Italy*. Empfindsamkeit refers to the sensitive and authentic experience of emotions and reached its literary climax in Germany with Goethe's novel *Die Leiden des jungen Werthers* (The Sufferings of Young Werthers) written in 1774.

Empfindsamkeit established the concept of the emotionally self-perceived bourgeois individual. In opposition to the predominance of the nobility and the clergy, emotionality was discussed as an immediate and thus authentic expression of individual personality. In this context, the emotional programmatic is "a fully-fledged ideology that emerges as the product and trigger of an upheaval, namely the decisive one of Western history: the replacement of the feudalist corporative state by bourgeois society" (cf. Hansen, 1989, p. 39, translation David Kergel). With Empfindsamkeit, the concept of an emotional self-evidence was established as part of arguments which discursively legitimized the bourgeois claim to cultural power. The requirement of the bourgeois subject's emotional self-realization was contrasted with the staging of one's status, which was publicly performed in noble and courtly circles by performative mechanisms of representation (cf. Hansen, 1989). Demarcating these mechanisms of representation, an emotional ethic unfolded that thematized the expression of the self-determined individual on an emotional level. Sensitive emotions elude the normative access of feudal society.

In literature, this process of cultural self-understanding is narratively negotiated. With Goethe's *Die Leiden des jungen Werthers* (1774) at the latest, literature became a battlefield in which the loving subject is placed in irreconcilable opposition to civil society. Goethe's choice of format in the epistolary novel reveals the predominance of subjectivity on a formal level; subjective experience manifests itself in a literary form of representation that focuses on the subject as a narrative instance. The demarcation logic of emotional discourse develops a dynamic that transcends the bourgeois demarcation lines against the nobility: the bourgeois emotional discourse transcends its socio-historical conditions by directing itself against the norms and conventions of bourgeois society itself. This happens exemplarily when Lotte decides against Werther in favor of a secure marriage – the monad of bourgeois relations – with Albert. The loving bourgeois individual does not stand in opposition to a feudal state order. The loving subject is now in conflict with the moral self-understanding discourses of bourgeois society. This example shows how the bourgeois recoding of symbolic order leads to an emancipation claim. This claim to emancipation leads beyond the symbolic order of bourgeois society itself – an aspect that we can also observe in the field of learning.

Note

1 https://worldhistorycommons.org/saint%E2%80%93just%E2%80%99s-speech-king%E2%80%99s-fate-27-december-1792 (accessed April 18, 2020).

Chapter 2

From emancipation to Erziehung and Bildung as Bourgeois educational theory and practice

The Latin verb *emancipare* originally denotes the dismissal of a slave or son from *mancipum* (possession) into independence. In the context of the social transformation which led to a new symbolic order, the notion of *emancipare* took a new meaning. Within the context of bourgeois self-understanding discourses, the term emancipation signifies the act of a guided self-liberation. The meaning of the adjective 'emancipative' can be thus defined as guidedly self-liberative. Within the pedagogical context, emancipation can be understood as an effect of pedagogical practice.

From an epistemological perspective, civil society is based on a voluntaristic-rational understanding of the subject, according to which the subject asserts itself independently of otherworldly instances. Education has the task of shaping the individual and thus creating a bourgeois emancipated subject.

In Germany's bourgeois culture and its tradition of pedagogical theory and practice there exists a distinction between *Erziehung* and *Bildung*. It is possible to translate both terms with the notion education. But this translation would mean a loss of meaning of the original German terms.

- Basically, Erziehung signifies the integration of the individual into the symbolic order of a society via pedagogical strategies.
- Bildung means the unfolding of the subject without pedagogical constraints. Both approaches deal on a pedagogical level with the freedom of the bourgeois subject.

While Bildung stresses the aspect of a self-determined unfolding of the subject, Erziehung focuses the integration of the bourgeois subject into the constraints and value-settings of civil society.

According to theoreticians on Erziehung like Kant or Durkheim, the individual has to be cultivated through Erziehung. Erziehung transforms the individual into a civilized human being. This means that the individual positions himself at a reflective distance to his natural needs. Erziehung means enculturation into a symbolic order via education. Through socialization processes the symbolic order reproduces itself performatively, inscribing the societal code within individuals in the course of a subjection process.[1] According to Durkheim, Erziehung is a specific form of socialization. As *guided* socialization, Erziehung creates the individual according to the symbolic structure of a society – including its values, morals, and ethics (cf. Durkheim, 1972).

The distinguishing trait of Erziehung is the distinction between nature and freedom: "Discipline changes animal nature into human* nature. Animals are by their instinct all that they ever can be; some other reason has provided everything for them at the outset. But man needs a reason of his own" (Kant, 1900, p. 2). The rational-based bourgeois subject is a cultivated subject. According to Kant, one feature of the bourgeois subject is the competence to overcome her own bodily needs:

> It is discipline, which prevents man from being turned aside by his animal impulses from humanity, his appointed end. Discipline, for instance, must restrain him from venturing wildly and rashly into danger. Discipline, thus, is merely negative, its action being to counteract man's natural unruliness. The positive part of education is instruction. Unruliness consists in independence of law. By discipline men are placed in subjection to the laws of mankind, and brought to feel their constraint.
>
> (Kant, 1900, p. 3)

According to Kant's concept of education, the freedom of the bourgeois subject is evident in the competence of rational self-reflection. This competence of rational self-reflection implies that the individual becomes accustomed to the constraints and duties of civil society: "By learning to think, man comes to act according to fixed principles and not at random" (Kant, 1900, p. 6). Two of the essential features of a bourgeois subject in a meritocratic civil society are discipline and industriousness. Thus, essential educational goals are discipline and the 'will to work':

> A child must play, must have his hours of recreation; but he must also learn to work. It is a good thing, doubtless, to exercise skill, as it is to cultivate the mind, but these two kinds of culture should have their separate hours. Moreover, it is a great misfortune for 'man that he is by nature so inclined to' inaction. The longer a man gives way to this inclination, the more difficult will he find it to make up his mind to work.
>
> (Kant, 1900, p. 68)

Such an educational strategy puts the subject into a position where he could unfold his "love of freedom" (Kant, 1900, p. 4). But to do so, the subject has to be accustomed to its freedom via Erziehung. Once the human being is accustomed to freedom, the subject "will sacrifice everything for its sake" (Kant, 1900, p. 4). But "[f]or this very reason discipline must be brought into play very early; for when this has not been done, it is difficult to alter character later in life. Undisciplined men are apt to follow every caprice" (Kant, 1900, p. 68).

2.1 Erziehung-constellation

With reference to this understanding of Erziehung as a specific kind of educational practice, Erziehung can be analyzed with the following elements:

- Erziehungsziel (Educational Goal)
- Erzieher (Educator)
- Zu-Erzieher (Educand).

The interplay of the three elements constitute a constellation (Erziehungkonstellation) in which the educand is defined as a deficit being. The educational goal represents a 'target state' which the educand should achieve. That means that the educand lacks something – for example, competence, a special way to behave. This lack of something is represented in the educational goal. Thus, an educational necessity defines the educand as a subject lacking competence that he should develop in the course of the Erziehungsprozess (educational process). The educator is the leading figure within this constellation. The educator has to ensure that the educand reaches the educational goal and thus overcomes his deficit state (Figure 2.1).

2.2 Erziehung and learning theory

Learning as a concept is discussed in the field of learning theories. Learning theories discuss the way learning is produced by its context and environment. Here, the way communication is organized and performed within learning

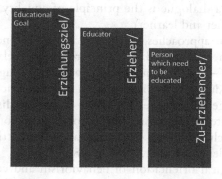

Figure 2.1 Erziehung as guided Socialization (into the Symbolic Order of Society). Erziehung can be analyzed in form of Erziehung-Constellation (own illustration).

contexts can be considered as the main difference between the leading learning theories – mainly between behaviorism, cognitivism, constructivism, and connectivism. Speaking about Erziehung in the field of learning, one can refer to the learning theories behaviorism and cognitivism.[2]

To transfer the educational concept of Erziehung into the field of learning, one can identify two learning strategies which match the criteria of Erziehung as a specific kind of educational practice:

- Cognitive learning via instructions and Learning to control emotions in order to develop the competencies to work with discipline and industriousness. The educator turns into the teacher and the educand becomes the learner.

Behavioristic conceptions of learning see the learning individual in a fairly passive role: the learning individual receives stimuli and develops stable reactions. The manifestation of these stable reactions can be considered the learning effect. Typical behaviorist strategies like positive reinforcement can be seen as a specific kind of communication practice. The positive feedback of a desired action fosters the desired behavior. Behavioristically oriented communication strategies aim to establish the intended behavior:

> A person learning to drive a car responds to the verbal behavior of the person sitting beside him; he starts, stops, shifts, signals, and so on when told to do so. [...] Much of education is instruction in verbal behavior. The student is told how to 'use words' rather how to use an accelerator; he is told how to behave.
>
> (Skinner, 2011, p. 134).

From this point of view, communication practice in behavioristically oriented conceptions is asymmetrical and thus not dialogical, at least when an essential feature of a dialogue is the principle of equality of all participants (even between teacher and learner).

As in behavioristic approaches, *cognitivistic conceptions* tend to cast the learning individual in a passive and receptive role. The relationship between teacher and learner – the communication partners – is again asymmetrical. The learning individual receives information from the teacher and is to transfer it into knowledge: "It requires a sensitive teacher to distinguish an intuitive mistake – an interesting wrong leap – from a stupid or ignorant mistake, and it requires a teacher who can give approval and correction simultaneously to the intuitive student" (Bruner, 2009, p. 68).

The epistemological orientation of behaviorism and cognitivism stresses the logical structure of the world. This logical structure of the world is to be internalized by the learning individual. The learning process has to be arranged in such a way as to enable the individual to acquire the objectively correct knowledge. In this sense, learning is normative. *Learning results can be identified as right or wrong*; it is important that the learner produces the 'right' knowledge. The teacher, as a communication partner, has to ensure that the learning individual receives this normatively right knowledge. From this point of view, behaviorism and cognitivism deal with a (more or less explicitly) asymmetrical communication structure: the teacher must guide the learner so that the learner can acquire the right knowledge. Due to their asymmetrical communicative orientation, behaviorism and cognitivism operate through a non-dialogical communication structure. In terms of Erziehung one could say the teacher is the educator, the learner the educand, and the educational goal is the learning goal. In other words, Erziehung is based on a behavioristic and cognitivistic way of learning.

2.3 The media ecology of Erziehung

The understanding of an Erziehung-based learning is basically a behavioristic/cognitive way of learning. The behavioristic/cognitive way of learning also has a media dimension. In the era when learning and education emerged within the civil society, the media ecology changed profoundly. Media ecology is a theoretical model developed by McLuhan (cf. McLuhan, 1964). As a way of analyzing the socio-historic dimensions of media in general, media ecology focuses on the history of media, technology, the way media is integrated into society, and the way media influences and changes culture and society as a whole:

> We put the word 'media' in the front of the word ‹ecology› to suggest that we were not simply interested in media, but in the ways in which the interaction between media and human beings give a culture its character and, one might say, help a culture to maintain symbolic balance. If we wish to connect the ancient meaning with the modern, we might say that the word suggests that we need to keep our planetary household in order.
>
> (Postman, 2000, p. 11)

According to Postman, media ecology is thus concerned with research of culturally constituent interactions between media and people, whereby this research is purposeful: it is concerned with maintaining a balanced budget of social ecology between people and technology.

Media would thus be understood in the ecological sense as the infrastructure of human actions but also including non-human actors. Media enable, force, and prevent connections. Media ecology recognizes that media constitutively determine our perceptions, our experiences, and our communication. On the other hand, new media unfold in an already existing socio-cultural (media) ecology, which is structured by 'old media.'

2.3.1 The birth of modern book culture

In the course of the 19th century and the liberal-democratic movement of civil society the press emerged as a discursive impact of the bourgeois emancipation movement. The development of civil society is inextricably linked with the development of letterpress printing. Johannes Gutenberg developed a moveable, mechanical type printing technology. Mechanical type printing enabled, at least potentially, an infinite reproduction of letters. The introduction of letterpress printing around 1450 (Johannes Gutenberg printed his first Latin Bible between 1450 and 1455) can be considered a disruptive process or a media revolution (cf. Eisenstein, 2005). Eisenstein speaks about a "long revolution" (Eisenstein, 2005, p. 335) between 1450 and 1470. In the course of this long revolution the book turns from a writing medium to a printing medium.

McLuhan states that the book and print technology provided a media foundation for civil society. This new media foundation had specific effects on social interaction "Print had a levelling function on all verbal and social forms" (McLuhan, 2011, p. 239). Due to the spread of printed books the idea of a cross-locational cultural identity and a national idea could spread. Literacy also increased (cf. Niedermair, 1992, p. 536). With increased literacy new forms of bourgeois culture could unfold. One effect of the establishment of the printing process was the model of the bourgeois author: the names of authors were shown on the title pages of books. Print technology and the model of the single, creative author led to the first copyright laws. The copyright was established in the USA in 1790, in France in 1793, and in Prussia in 1837. The copyright laws constituted the author as a legal person (cf. Dommann, 2008, p. 44).

2.3.2 The rebellion of the printed word

According to McLuhan, print media created national uniformity and fostered the centralized government. But with print technology arose new forms of individualism and opposition to the government (McLuhan, 2011, p. 235). The printing of books raised concerns about possible negative impacts of the printing press as new media. In particular, the clergy feared that the Enlightenment and the Reformation could undermine the symbolic order and established powers like the Catholic Church. A decay of morals could be one of the effects and the cultural impacts of the printing press. Censorship and persecution were the consequences. The Catholic Church installed the papal bull *Inter Multiplices* as a tool for censorship in 1487. This censorship was mainly directed against the ideas of Humanism, the Enlightenment, and the Reformation. The Lateran Council affirmed the papal bull *Inter Multiplices* in 1515. The ecclesiastical imprimatur was a prerequisite for the legal printing of writings concerning the faith. This legitimized the censorship of works of theological teaching, literature, the fine arts, and the performing arts. Authors could be prosecuted with a ban on teaching, persecution, or even execution. On the other hand, the Catholic Church used the printing press to produce illustrated Bibles.

The concerns of the Catholic Church were legitimate fears: printing allowed the genre of leaflets as a forum for rebellion and criticism of authority. The Reformation used leaflets to vernacularize its positions (Eisenstein, 2005, p. 208; Faulstich, 2004, p. 145). According to Faulstich (2004), approximately three billion leaflets were disseminated in Germany in 1524. Besides the leaflets, newspapers were relevant 'mouthpieces' of social transformations.

The phenomenon of the newspaper emerged at the end of the 17th century against the background of an increased need for information as civil society developed. As a medium of 'relevant news,' newspapers possessed political significance from the very beginning. With the newspaper a bourgeois public formed against the culture of the feudal nobility.

The dynamic of bourgeois revolutions like the American War of Independence or the French Revolution were deeply influenced by newspapers. In 1770, American newspapers reported the 'massacres of the English army' – for example, the so-called Boston Massacre.[3] Leading political activist like John Adams, who was George Washington's successor, used writing as a forum. And the so-called Federalist Papers supported the ratification of the Constitution. It is no wonder that the Bill of Rights guaranteed the freedom of the press (First Amendment for freedom of speech which was ratified in 1791).

In the course of the French Revolution, newspapers like the Le Révolutions de Paris were printed. It is estimated that in the first years of the French Revolution, nearly 300 newspapers emerged (Reichardt, 2008, p. 234). These were often 'mouthpieces' of political parties. But with Napoleon Bonaparte's rule freedom of the press was limited and the press was monitored by the so-called bureau de la presse.

The printed word was/is part of the bourgeois culture. It was/is the medium of its self-understanding discourses and thus involved in political debates. Just as the leaflet and the newspaper held meaning for the public sphere of civil society, the printed book became the medium of bourgeois epistemological thinking.

2.3.3 The book as media of autonomous and rational thinking

Basically, one could propose the thesis that printed texts foster individual reflection (cf. Reckwitz, 2012). In consequence, texts were created that represented personal confessions – for example, texts of Empfindsamkeit or Jean Jacques Rousseau's famous *Confessions*.

> I have entered upon a performance which is without example, whose accomplishment will have no imitator. I mean to present my fellow-mortals with a man in all the integrity of nature; and this man shall be

myself. I know my heart, and have studied mankind; I am not made like any one I have been acquainted with, perhaps like no one in existence; if not better, I at least claim originality, and whether Nature did wisely in breaking the mould with which she formed me, can only be determined after having read this work. Whenever the last trumpet shall sound, I will present myself before the sovereign judge with this book in my hand.

(Rouuseau, n.d., p. 9)

The bourgeois individual is the 'typographic man:' The printing enabled a discourse of the 'written word:' The book substituted the oral and potentially holistic dialogue between two individuals. It is no wonder, that almost all relevant modern intellectual debates of civil society base on the printed word. The book became the symbol of knowledge – and still today, intellectuals are portraited in front of bookshelves.

Cognitive knowledge is mediated via the printed words of the books. Discursive feedback is also provided via printed words. Authors could refer to each other in their writings. One current example of this technique is citation systems like American Psychological Association.

The linear structure of the book, the syntagmatic structure of the written word, fosters analytical-linear thinking. Following this thought, one can conclude that the printed words are an abstract mediation of knowledge. From this perspective, the book fosters abstract thinking and rational argumentation. Using the written word, the scholar unfolds his rational thinking. The printed book and the authorship turn into symbols and media of free, autonomous, and rational thinking. Still today, the author of scientific book is considered a member of the scientific community and a bachelor's thesis can be considered the entry into the scientific community.

2.3.4 Learning in the book culture

From the middle of the 17th century onwards, educators thought intensively and systematically about the possibilities of the book for learning purposes. It was discussed how reading and writing could be taught with the help of books. The first fibulas and reading books were written to teach both language and reading skills, as well as knowledge in general. In 1658, Comenius published the volume *Orbis sensulium pictus*. This volume contained illustrations and texts in Latin and German and became a classic in the field of learning books. The book became increasingly important for learning.

The semiotic structure of books will be analyzed below against this background of book's importance for learning in the emerging bourgeois society.

With the Gutenberg Galaxy, "the dynamic logic of printing as a centralizing and homogenizing force" (McLuhan, 2011, p. 230) emerged. This led to the concept of the individual author who creates literature and distributes knowledge through the publication of their books. Barthes points out the historical conditions which gave rise to this concept:

> The author is a modern figure, a product of our society insofar as, emerging from the Middle Ages with English empiricism, French rationalism and the personal faith of the Reformation, it discovered the prestige of the individual, of, as it is more nobly put, the 'human person.' It is thus logical that in literature it should be this positivism, the epitome and culmination of capitalist ideology, which has attached the greatest importance to the 'person' of the author.
>
> (Barthes, 2008, p. 313)

From a perspective of educational theory, the author can be analyzed as the teacher while the recipient is the learner: In the academic field, the scholarly author represents the emancipated, active citizen who constructs rationally based knowledge with their writings. The scholarly author produces knowledge and disseminates it through books. The concept of the author establishes a scholarly hierarchy, which is defined by the poles of writing and reading. The author represents one pole: he writes the book. The unidirectional orientation of the printed book performatively reproduces the poles of reading and writing. The structure of the printed book requires a sharp distinction between author and reader. The author provides knowledge through his written text and printed book. But the author needs a reader. In academia, the author communicates his knowledge via books and journals.

The "order of the book" (Weel, 2011, p. 91) and the concept of the scholarly author also influences learning. In the Gutenberg Galaxy, learning is based on the distinction between the author and the reader, who can be considered the 'learner:' "The printed book was a new visual aid available to all students and it rendered the older education obsolete. The book was literally a teaching machine" (McLuhan, 2011, p. 164). The student reading a book became an iconic representation of study. The asymmetric relation between the author as teacher and the reader as learner mirrors the relation of education. As a specific kind of educational practice, reading can be analyzed via the elements in the structure of Erziehung.

- Erziehungsziel (Educational Goal): The Erziehungsziel is that the educand acquires knowledge via reading a book.
- Erzieher (Educator): The author is the Erzieher because through her book she mediates the knowledge represented in the Erziehungsziel.
- Zu-Erziehende (Educand): The Zu-Erziehende is the reader. He needs to acquire the knowledge which is written down in the book he is reading (Figure 2.2).

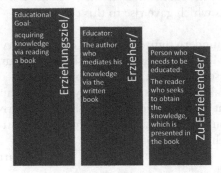

Figure 2.2 Visualization of the medial Erziehung-Constellation within the Gutenberg Galaxy's Book Culture (own illustration).

The way the book is structured, or the way the knowledge is presented (e.g., with tables, pictures, etc.), structures the way the Zu-Erziehende acquires the knowledge. Thus, the author presents not solely his knowledge. He is also a 'didactician' because he defines how the reader receives the knowledge. With the asymmetric relation between the author and the reader in this learning context a cognitivist way of learning is established. The logical structure of the world is discovered by the scientists of the world and disseminated in the written language of the world.

The linear, syntagmatic structure of the written language conveys the logical structures of the world. This basic media structure manifests itself exemplarily in the book.

2.4 Bildung in the book culture of civil society

The German notion of Bildung is one of the most prominent concepts in continental education: "*Bildung* is one of the fundamental concepts of modernity and the most ambiguous concept of German pedagogy, providing a range of uses and interpretations" (Alves, 2019, para. 3, emphasis in original.; cf. Fuhr, Laros, & Taylor, 2017, p. ix).

It is often stressed that Bildung is above all a phenomenon of the German language and has no literal translation into English: "*Bildung* is a specifically German coinage for which it is extraordinar- it is difficult to find equivalents in other languages. For this reason, literal renderings or awkward descriptions are necessary in neighboring languages in order to clarify what Bildung is" (Koselleck, 2002, p. 173, emphasis in original).

But already in antiquity a distinction was made between *educatio* (rearing: discipline, civilization) and *eruditio* (cultivation of the soul and the spirit). This distinction can be understood as the first anticipation of the distinction between Bildung and Erziehung. However, the epistemological understanding of Bildung is closely linked to the philosophy of German idealism and is still a powerful legacy of this philosophical epoch.[4]

In the search for the concept of Bildung, the understanding of Bildung as developed within German idealism is helpful. The answer to this question requires a historically trained approach. Like Erziehung, the development of Bildung as a pedagogical concept – and above all Bildung as understood within German idealism – is closely linked to the emergence of civil society. German idealism developed an epistemological understanding of the human being. This understanding can be considered the philosophical foundation of bourgeois culture: as a citizen, the individual is an active subject.[5] Unlike the nobleman who owes his social status to birth, the bourgeois citizen earns her own reputation within the society. This concept of the citizen corresponds to a philosophical understanding of the individual which is defined by the fact that the individual creates his self-world relation by engaging with the world. The voluntaristic version of the active citizen is also reflected in the philosophical understanding of idealism. Idealism refers to a form of knowledge acquisition which goes beyond sensual seeing and the external, concrete reality. The term 'ideal' means that the construction/perception of the world does not stop at externalities (cf. Ludwig, 2009, p. 18). In acting within the world and as part of the world, we develop an 'idea' of the world. According to this epistemological premise, a basic thesis of German idealism is that our knowledge and our experience of the world are also shaped by an immanent intellectual development (cf. Bubner, 2004, p. 17). In the most radical positions of German idealism (e.g., Fichte), all reality is only an idea of the ego, which the ego gains from the confrontation with the world.

Another figure of thought that distinguishes German idealism from other epistemological approaches is the coincidence of subject and object. The philosophy of German idealism thinkers like Schelling is guided by the philosophical project of 'thinking the unity/merging of subject and object' (cf. Bubner, 2004, p. 18). The subject is not isolated from the world as an object. Rather, the subject is inseparably connected to the world and part of the world. This epistemological position which is strongly represented by Hegel and Schelling (cf. Kergel, 2011) is also a characteristic feature of Humboldt's theory on Bildung. Like Hegel, Humboldt conceptualize the cognitive process of the subject as an infinite becoming of the subject. To define this process Humboldt, like Hegel, uses the term Bildung. Through Bildung, man constructs a relationship between himself and the world. "Bildung is cultivation of the self by the self" (Laros, Fuhr, Laros & Taylor, 2017, p. ix). In other words, Humboldt understands Bildung as a process of holistic cognition through which the subject develops a concept of the world and of herself. In the moment the subject identifies himself as a part of the world, the subject identifies himself as an individual part of humanity:

> It is the ultimate task of our existence to achieve as much substance as possible for the concept of humanity in our person, both during the span of our life and beyond it, through the traces we leave by means of our

vital activity. This can be fulfilled only by the linking of the self to the world to achieve the most general, most animated, and most unrestrained interplay.

(Humboldt, 2000, p. 58)

According to Humboldt, enlightenment and idealism are closely related to each other – especially in the matter of Bildung (cf. Lauer, 2017, p. 242). In Humboldt's understanding of Bildung manifests the bourgeois cultural claim to power; with the cultural establishment of civil society, Hegel and Humboldt reinterpreted and revitalized the concept of Bildung which already possessed a long tradition: In its origins the term Bildung actually had a sacred meaning. The sacred meaning originates from German mysticism in the Middle Ages. Originally, the word Bildung possessed an 'active meaning' and signified the creation and forming of things like a sculpture or a potter (cf. Koselleck, 2006, p. 113). In the course of German mysticism, the term Bildung and its meaning were transferred to the sphere of mystic 'spiritual creation'; since the 14th century, Bildung signified a mystically oriented epistemology. Consequently, the epistemological origins of the German concept of Bildung are to be found in the German mysticism of the 14th century. Mystical experiences are subjective-spiritual experiences that are inaccessible by language and are a subjective experience of God. Via Bildung, a 'God-likeness' of the human being could be reached. As mentioned before, in Old High German *Bildunga* signified the creative production of things like pots. The term Bildung was chosen to translate the Latin word *imago* from the history of creation, thus giving the originally concrete term *Bildunga* a transcendent meaning (cf. Horlacher, 2011, p. 17):

> The German word *bilden* contains an active meaning, namely of creating and forming, which is discernible in "molding" *(Bildnerei)*, for example that of a potter; this meaning also became applicable to spiritual creation. However, since the fourteenth century, the term also refers, in theological context, to a more passive, certainly reception-oriented meaning that *comes* from creation theology. "God created human beings in his image *(Bilde)*."9 From this followed the possibility of *imitatio Christi* or the *imago Dei* doctrine, or the requirement of Neoplatonism that the copy *(Ab-bild)* approach the original *(Urbild)*. The language of mysticism evoked a wealth of locutions, still primarily verbal ones: *Entbilden* (to deform), *einbilden* (to imagine), and *überbilden* (to transfigure) are steps in the dissolution from earthly reality in order to fuse together God and the soul.
>
> (Koselleck, 2002, p. 176)

When Bildung became a basic concept of bourgeois thinking, the shift of meaning of the word Bildung also signified an epistemological shift (cf. Kergel, 2019). The modern, bourgeois concept of Bildung is deprived of any sacred connotation – the bourgeois concept of Bildung no longer knows anything divine. According to Humboldt, Bildung manifests itself in subject's inner need to unfold herself. Accordingly, Bildung is not the expression of the mystic desire of imitating external transcendent models such as God.

In short, it can be stated that within the pedagogy of the Enlightenment Bildung was detached from theological and mystical contexts. In the course of the bourgeois self-understanding discourse the term Bildung was revitalized and became a key word for the bourgeois process of emancipation. In a bourgeois version of Bildung, the subject unfolds just like the civil citizen unfolds through active engagement *in* the world and *with* the world. The bourgeois individual recognizes the world through active action – not through contemplative reflection. Thus, the modern, enlightened, and bourgeois human being does not find his happiness in rest but in activity (cf. Musloff, 1989, p. 119). Thus, one characteristic feature of Bildung is an activist concept of the subject, who engages within the world and thus unfolds herself. This activist concept of the subject bears potential for pedagogical approaches.

The subject acquires knowledge about the world as an active citizen. Even if Bildung is based on knowledge and always includes the production and the acquisition of knowledge, Bildung is more than just the adoption of knowledge.

> The first function of the classical ideal of *Bildung* is integration by education and culture. This function is associated with the normative notion of humanity and the idea of an integral individual as a unifying and totalizing instance. Humanism as normative ideal places itself above social bodies, sexes, religious denominations and nations. Thus, to form oneself, to educate means to reconnect to the image of humanity within itself.
>
> (Alves, 2019, para. 4)

As a process, Bildung aims to produce knowledge as an manifestation of an active self and world relationship (cf. Ricken, 2006, p. 321, footnote): "In pure, ultimate terms, thought is never more than an attempt of the mind to be comprehensible to itself, whereas action is an attempt of the will to become free and independent in itself" (Humboldt, 2000, p. 58). This process in which the subject produces *knowledge* about herself and about the world is driven by the 'power' of the human being. According to Humboldt, this cognitive process is defined by an experiential dimension that results from the interaction of power and 'freedom.' The subject needs spaces of freedom to experience himself in the course of his *Bildungsprozess* (Bildung-Process):

> He sees that, executed in the right way, his business will give the mind its own, fresh view of the world and through this its own, fresh self-determination, so that he can achieve a full measure of Bildung from this, his own perspective; it is this he strives to achieve. If, however, he works

only for power and its enhancement, he may satisfy himself only when he expresses his own power perfectly in his work.

(Humboldt, 2000, p. 60)

Power and freedom are central concepts of Humboldt's theory on Bildung, so it is worth taking a closer look at the two concepts.

Humboldt adapted the concept of power from the natural philosophy discourses of his time. Natural philosophy discussed how nature unfolds as matter without any influence from the divine: power and matter were the new basic concepts. Natural events were explained without the hypothesis of a god and solely with the help of the thesis of cause–effect relationships.

As part of nature, the human being is also driven by a natural power. Plants, animals, and humans are driven by the power of nature. The process of forming oneself is the manifestation of an innate power that permeates all nature. Just as a plant grows and unfolds its power the human being unfolds her power in her engagement with the world. The subject receives stimuli from outside, absorbs these stimuli into his interior, and thus forms himself (*bilden*/forming) into a harmonious whole:

> However, because sheer power needs an object on which it may be exercised and pure form or idea needs a material in which, expressing itself, it can last, so too does man need a world outside himself. From this springs his endeavor to expand the sphere of his knowledge and his activity, and without himself being clearly aware of it, he is not really concerned with what he obtains from the former or what he achieves outside himself by means of the latter, but only with his inner improvement and elevation, or at least with the appeasement of the inner unrest that consumes him.
>
> (Humboldt, 2000, p. 58)

Engaging in the world and acting within the world means at the same time changing the world.

> Man's entire external activity is nothing but the striving against futility. Simply because both his thought and his action are not possible except by means of a third element, the representation and cultivation of something that is actually characterized by being non-man, that is, world, he seeks to grasp as much world as possible and bind it as tightly as he can to himself.
>
> (Humboldt, 2010, p. 58)

This process can primarily be understood as a means of Self-Bildung (*Selbst-Bildung*/self-forming). Self-Bildung is a matter of freedom. In this context, freedom signifies the concrete process by which the subject chooses in an intentional act the way of life appropriate to the unfolding of her individuality (cf. Musolff, 1989, p. 125). The human being needs free spaces which allow him to unfold his power self-determinedly. The development of power is inseparably linked to freedom; in order to engage *with* and *within* world and thus unfold her force, the subject needs freedom:

> It is often enough underscored that self-formation (Selbstbildung) through sociability had an emancipatory function because it was directed against all authorities, because it constituted itselfoutside the state, and be- cause it openly positioned itselfagainst differences of social estate and pre-vailing ecclesiastical precepts.
>
> (Koselleck, 2002, p. 182)

2.4.1 The media ecology of Bildung

The bourgeois individual is defined by self-awareness and self-reflection: The bourgeois individual unfolds via hermeneutical perspective on himself. The media for this hermeneutical self-observation is the writing system. Thus, the bourgeois individual is represented in the first person singular – the 'I.' Through writing the bourgeois individual unfolds herself and the world in which she is embedded. According to the epistemological premises of the German Idealism the subject (re-)constructs the world via reflection. This (re-)construction is mostly inward – like reading and writing. Reading and writing in noiseless solitude contradict the nobitility's public staging of lit-erature. Inward reading and writing create a private space. This corresponds with the emergence of text genres such as biographies, autobiographies, and diaries. These text genres represent the concept that the individual is the master of his own life. When writing a text, the bourgeois individual un-folds themself as a self (and thus turns into a subject).[6] In reading biogra-phies and autobiographies the bourgeois individual reflects psychological experiences.

Reading and writing are cultural practices in which the bourgeois self un-folds. The concept of a coherent self which could narrate itself coherently has its foundation in these self-technologies of writing and reading. Bourgeois reading and writing are inextricably linked. They provide a form of inner experience and lead to the dominance of visual cultures.[7]

The bourgeois individual is a reading and writing individual, at least when the individual writes letters or diary entries. This forms in turn a specific kind of (self-)attentiveness in everyday life.[8] This self-attentiveness is also a characteristic feature of Bildung. First of all, Bildung is a kind of world-related self-awareness. To foster this self-awareness is a project which is

> limited to man's inner being, his nature drives him to reach beyond himself to the external objects, and here it is crucial that he should not lose himself in this alienation, but rather reflect back into his inner being

the clarifying light and the comforting warmth of everything that he undertakes outside himself.

(Humboldt, 2000, p. 59)

This reflection process can be achieved and materialized via writing. Writing is thus a sequential structuring of the world. In the linearity of writing, the world is ordered in a linear way.

> Man seeks unity only to escape from dissipating and confusing diversity. In order not to become lost in infinity, empty and unfruitful, he creates a single circle, visible at a glance from any point. In order to attach the image of the ultimate goal to every step forward he takes, he seeks to transform scattered knowledge and action into a closed system, mere scholarship into scholarly Bildung, merely restless endeavor into judicious activity.

(Humboldt, 2000, p. 60)

Through reading and writing the bourgeois individual and social reality unfold in a logical order. This applies to world history as well as the biography of the individual. The medium of this process is written text. This approach is based on the assumption of the 'readability of the world.' The world can be conquered through reading and writing. One example is the "Encyclopédie ou Dictionnaire raisonné des sciences, des arts et des métiers" (*Encyclopedia, or a Systematic Dictionary of the Sciences, Arts, and Crafts*).[9] The encyclopedia became a symbol against the authority of traditional knowledge. The acquisition of knowledge – a fundamental feature of learning – becomes a bourgeois virtue. Another example for the superiority of the text is the so-called 'armchair-ethnography.'[10]

The expanding world of civil society and bourgeois culture is also a world of expanding texts. The texts in turn represent the *Bildungsstand* (the level of Bildung) of a society.

2.4.2 The dialogical dimension of Bildung and the emergence of the public sphere

The epistemological starting point of Bildung is the single individual. In its deeper structure Bildung can be analyzed as a collaborative process. The single individual engages with the world. This world is a social world in which the individual is embedded. The individual constructs her knowledge about the world by engaging within the world. Engaging in the world means engaging with other individuals. In this *intersubjective* dimension, Bildung can be considered as a dialogically oriented process. Referring to the Greek origins of the notion dialogue, *dia* signifies a distance as well as a process (cf. Jullien, 2017).

- The distance can be considered as the distance between the dialogue partners.
- In a communication process, the dialogue partners exchange their points of views. Within this exchange process, the dialogue partners move their perspectives and thus reduce the distance between each other. In this movement process, a new and now common understanding of a phenomenon is constructed.

The dialogue can be understood as the ideal concept of democratic communication within civil society: the individual undergoes a Bildung-Process by engaging in and with the world dialogically.

On a supra-individual level, the civil society undergoes a Bildung-Process via the dialogical exchange within the so-called bourgeois public sphere. The concept of the bourgeois public sphere corresponds with the flourishing newspaper market:

> The *bourgeois public sphere* could be understood as the sphere of private individuals assembled into a public body, which almost immediately laid claim to the officially regulated "intellectual newspapers" for use against the public authority itself. In those newspapers, and in moralistic and critical journals, they debated that public authority on the general rules of social intercourse in their fundamentally privatized yet publicly relevant sphere of labor and commodity exchange.
> (Habermas, Lennox, & Lennox, 1964, p. 52, emphasis in original)

From this point of view, the public sphere is the medium to construct public opinion.[11] In this context, Bildung can be interpreted as the epistemological foundation of Western discourse-culture: Bildung is a manifestation of the bourgeois individual's self-determination and his claim to freedom. One feature of freedom of the bourgeois individual is the capability to think her own thoughts. The development of this capability is part of the Bildung-Process and unfolds within the discursive landscape of the public sphere. The public sphere is the medium in which the dialogical process takes place on a public level. Because Bildung unfolds within the public sphere, Bildung can be analyzed as a dialogical process.

This thesis corresponds with the development of the newspaper sector. Before 1798, journalists were more like chroniclers. Since the French Revolution, journalists have seen themselves as advocates for the people and as political actors (cf. Kergel, 2020). In the French Revolution, newspapers were platforms for political parties. Although censorship was introduced in the French Revolution of 1792, the concept of the bourgeois newspaper was 'in the world.' The freedom of the press was restricted out of fear of revolutions – especially with the beginning of the restoration phase in 1815.[12] (Bourgeois) emancipation, the press, and protests are interconnected – until our current time. Bildung in turn can be considered an important part of the epistemological foundation of the emancipation of the bourgeois individual.

2.4.3 Between Bildung and Erziehung: ambivalence of the public sphere

The relationship between Bildung and Erziehung reflects a structural ambivalence of civil society. On one hand, there is the emancipation of the individual – represented by the concept of Bildung. On the other, there is bourgeois society as a functional structure in which every citizen has his place – represented by the concept of Erziehung. This structural ambivalence also raises the question of the possibilities and limits of self-determination in the context of civil society. Kant thematized this ambivalence and its potential for conflicts in the 1784 published essay "Answering the Question: What is Enlightenment?".

Kant's essay contains a number of points that are significant for his understanding of the relationship between the individual's freedom and the normative, rationally based demands of civil society. Kant elaborated a concept that describes how a rationally based society is to be organized so that it creates the possibility of self-enlightenment as a process. In the course of this process, civil society reproduces itself quasi-autopoietically. "It is more nearly possible, however, for the public to enlighten itself" (Kant, n.d., para. 3).[13]

Kant's concept bears pedagogical implications and can be interpreted as Kant's contribution to social education. His approach is based on the distinction between a public and a private use of reason. Another aspect is Kant's understanding of social practice as a practice that reproduces itself performatively and is set in analogy to a machine.

> In some affairs affecting the interest of the community a certain [governmental] mechanism is necessary in which some members of the community remain passive. This creates an artificial unanimity which will serve the fulfillment of public objectives, or at least keep these objectives from being destroyed. Here arguing is not permitted: one must obey [...] Thus it would be very unfortunate if an officer on duty and under orders from his superiors should want to criticize the appropriateness or utility of his orders. He must obey.
>
> (Kant, n.d., para. 6)[14]

To ensure the functioning of the 'machine civil society' the individual has to obey. But the public sphere can be used to raise questions concerning legitimacy of the regulations:

> But as a scholar he could not rightfully be prevented from taking notice of the mistakes in the military service and from submitting his

views to his public for its judgment. The citizen cannot refuse to pay the taxes levied upon him; indeed, impertinent censure of such taxes could be punished as a scandal that might cause general disobedience. Nevertheless, this man does not violate the duties of a citizen if, as a scholar, he publicly expresses his objections to the impropriety or possible injustice of such levies. A pastor, too, is bound to preach to his congregation in accord with the doctrines of the church which he serves, for he was ordained on that condition. But as a scholar he has full freedom, indeed.

(Kant, n.d., para. 6)[15]

The results of public discourse can be transformed into a legal framework. Thus, civil society can enlighten itself. Enlightenment is a discursive project and in modern terms can be understood as 'organizational learning.' Through the private use of reason in the public discourse, critically secured knowledge can be generated, which in turn can be implemented in social practice. Through this process, knowledge is produced (analogous to the capitalist 'self-sustained growth'). The establishment of the discourse landscape is reflected in the establishment of the newspaper market. The newspaper market represents the societal self-enlightenment based in the public sphere. The self-enlightenment process of the public sphere is part of a societal Bildung-Process. Thus, Bildung can be conceptualized on an individual level and on a societal level. By participating in the discourse, civil society educates itself through rational discourse. This educational measure requires a separation of the individual into a

- **functional dimension** (the social role in the structure of the 'machine bourgeois society') and a
- **discursive dimension** (as part of the public sphere).

This division of the individual can be seen as an attempt to deal with the ambivalences of the bourgeoisie's emancipative concept of reason and the state's cultural-political claim to hegemony. With the introduction of the dichotomy of private and public use of reason, Kant divides the social individual into two spheres (cf. Kergel, 2013). In this way, social stability and rational practice are made possible at the same time: the citizen can reliably fulfill his duties and thus enable the machine-like functioning of the state. At the same time, discourse spaces of rational critique are enabled. On the basis of such discourse spaces rational critique and therewith a process of (self-)enlightenment can take place.

In summary, it can be stated that the relationship between self-determination and obedience constitutes a structural ambivalence of bourgeois society. In the pedagogical field, this ambivalence can be seen in the distinction between Bildung and Erziehung.

2.4.4 The empirical dimension of bildung

The concept of Bildung describes the activity and (self-)educational processes of the bourgeois individual on an epistemological and pedagogical level.[16] This section discusses how the central aspects of Bildung can be transferred into the field of empirical research. On this basis it is possible to conceptualize concrete strategies for the educational practice – which can also be applied in the digital age (see Section 5.9).

Mattig (2019) points out that Humboldt was not a purely theoretical thinker but also an empirical researcher. The separation between Bildung theory and empirical education research did not apply to Humboldt (according to Mattig, Humboldt was mainly active as an ethnographer.) Against the background of these considerations, the combination of educational theory and empirical research seems to be a logical step.

This approach requires that terms such as 'power' and 'freedom,' which Humboldt developed in the course of his theoretical considerations, can be used for concrete empirical educational practice.

The anthropological drive, which Humboldt defines as power and which forms the basis of Bildung, can be linked to the concept of exploration, or explorative curiosity. Exploration can be interpreted as an innate anthropological constant – without explorative curiosity the cognitive and emotional development of the individual is inconceivable. Exploration is manifested in a curious, explorative approach towards the world (cf. Gibson, 1998). With reference to Humboldt, explorative curiosity can be understood as a manifestation of the power that drives Bildung as a process. With regard to early childhood research, the development of explorative curiosity requires spaces of possibility. In the course of attachment style research, it was observed that children who had a secure bond were more likely to be explorative. Children with safe attachment behavior seemed to know that the attached person is available when needed for emotional coping. From this perspective, explorative curiosity is the result of a positive emotional relationship between self and world: the curious child is aware of the security in the world through her caregiver. This security enables a space in which explorative curiosity can unfold. In other words: The unfolding of exploration depends on the social context and its emotional implications. Manifestations of intrinsic motivations, such as interests, excitement, and a desire for challenges, are forms in which explorative curiosity unfolds. Learning in the sense of Bildung should entail such features.

While power finds its conceptual equivalence in the concept of explorative curiosity, the concept of freedom finds its equivalent in the concept of self-efficacy. With reference to Bandura (1977), self-efficacy can be interpreted as the conviction that appropriate behavioral outcomes can be achieved in a challenging situation. Perceived self-efficacy signifies the expectation that one's own competencies are sufficient to cope with a situation.

The strength of people's convictions in their own effectiveness is likely to affect whether they will even try to cope with given situations. At this initial level, perceived self-efficacy influences choice of behavioral settings. People fear and tend to avoid threatening situations they believe exceed their coping skills, whereas they get involved in activities and behave assuredly when they judge themselves capable of handling situations that would otherwise be intimidating. Not only can perceived self-efficacy have directive influence on choice of activities and settings, but, through expectations of eventual success, it can affect coping efforts once they are initiated.

(Bandura, 1977, S. 193f.)

The learning subject experiences himself as self-effective in the social context. In engaging with the world, the individual is able to unfold her explorative curiosity. In summary, it can be said that Bildung's mode of experience is represented

- by power and freedom from a Bildung-theoretical perspective and
- by explorative curiosity and perceived self-efficacy from an empirical-social-research perspective.

From the perspective of communication theories, one could add that power and freedom as well as explorative curiosity and perceived self-efficacy are embedded in dialogical structures. On the basis of these considerations it is possible to outline key points of Bildung-oriented didactics.

2.4.5 Bildung-oriented didactics

In Europe's civil society, the issue of didactics is originally tied to enlightenment and its pedagogy.[17] Enlightenment-based pedagogy stressed the development of reason. As critical citizens, the people should give themselves reasonable laws instead of being governed by church and king. In order to uncover and foster the potential of reason and rational thinking, adolescents should practice independent thinking and judgment. Most of the didactic models are in this tradition, including Bildung-oriented didactics.

Didactically guided teaching and learning is also an epistemological practice. Knowledge is generated in didactically framed learning processes. The decision for a certain way of teaching and learning mirrors a whole world view. Dalsgard (2005) elaborates on this relationship between theory and practice in learning and teaching.

A learning theoretical approach is developed on the basis of a philosophical understanding of knowledge and learning. A learning theory can be defined as *a conception of the individual, the world, the individual's relation to the world, and knowledge.* Analytically, learning principles can be divided into the form, content and relations of a learning environment. The concept of form describes the organization of the students' work; *how* do the students work with the subject matter? Content describes organization of the subject matter; *what* are the students working with? Finally, the concept of relations describes the relationship between the participants (teachers and students) in the learning environment and their respective roles. Learning principles can be defined as *an approach to form, content and relations of the learning environment.*

(Dalsgaard, 2005, Abs. 2, emphasis in original)

According to Dalsgard, "a learning theoretical approach is developed on the basis of a philosophical understanding of knowledge and learning. A learning theory can be defined as a conception of the individual, the world, the individual's relation to the world, and knowledge" (Dalsgaard, 2005, para. 1). Dalsgaard outlines the relationship between learning theory, basic didactic considerations and learning processes in a scheme (Figure 2.3).

The decision for a didactic model is also a value-driven decision (Reich, 2012). From this perspective learning and teaching are also ethical practices. The decision to elaborate on a Bildung-oriented didactic approach is a decision to foster the emancipative dimension within bourgeois epistemological and bourgeois pedagogical culture.

The following section introduces the key points of a Bildung-oriented didactic. A Bildung-oriented didactic follows the tradition of civil society's concept of the individual freedom. Within social contexts. Bildung represents the bourgeois freedom potential in the pedagogical field. Bildung-oriented didactics develops strategies to realize these freedom potentials within the teaching and learning process.

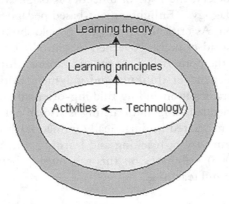

Figure 2.3 The relationship between learning theory, basic didactic considerations, and learning (Dalsgard, 2005, para. 9).

Despite the criticism of prescriptive handouts and the lack of theoretical depth of didactic models, the transfer into pedagogical practice remains a central challenge of didactics. In order to meet this challenge, an 'e-didactic criteria checklist' based on theoretical and empirical criteria was developed (cf. Kergel, 2019; Kergel & Heidkamp, 2015). This e-didactic criteria checklist specifically differs from instructional design (ID) models, which shape the didactic discussion in e-learning, especially in the Anglo-American region.

The model of ID goes back to Robert Gagné and is initially rooted in military training. ID, sometimes also ID or didactic design, refers to the systematic conception and provision of digital and physical learning environments. The starting point is the cognitivist conception of learning needs in order to develop teaching/learning scenarios on this basis. The planning and provision of teaching/learning scenarios are primarily based on a cognitivist understanding of learning and was linked to computer-based or digital forms of teaching from the earliest days.

The ID thus functions as a 'planning science' (cf. Seel, 1999). In this context, learning needs, the teaching/learning infrastructure and resources, are analyzed in order to design and provide a teaching/learning environment on their basis.

There are identifiable phases which generally shape project work but are also important for ID: Analysis, planning, development, implementation, and evaluation. The ADDIE model – an acronym for analysis phase, design phase, development phase, implementation phase, and evaluation phase – is one of the most common process descriptions for the creation of IDs. These phases are briefly outlined as follows:

- In the analysis phase, the teaching challenges are defined, the teaching objectives set, and the existing knowledge and skills of the learners identified.
- The design phase is dedicated to the planning of the teaching/learning design. This includes the planning of didactic learning paths, which should lead to the achievement of the learning objectives.
- In the development phase, the teaching/learning design, including the planned learning paths, will be further developed as they were conceived in the design phase.
- The implementation phase tests the practical suitability and prepares teachers for the teaching/learning situation or the course of the teaching/learning design – this preparation includes training in the use of digital tools. This phase also examines whether the technical-didactical infrastructure is ready for use.
- The evaluation phase runs crosswise to the other phases as a formatting process. After the other phases have been completed, the teaching/learning design is also subjected to summative evaluation.

The ID-based teaching/learning scenarios are run through by the learners. Especially in distance learning, where standardized forms of teaching and learning are used, IDs can contain added value. At least in its early days, distance learning was a streamlined and division-of-labor method of imparting knowledge. One challenge was to make it possible for a large number of learners, regardless of their place of residence, to learn/ teach the same things. It is not surprising that the spontaneity and unpredictability of learning cannot be taken into account as adequately in this cognitivist-plan-scientific approach. It is precisely on this spontaneity and unpredictability of learning that Bildung and socio-constructivist theories are based, which consequently stand in a certain tension with the didactic understanding of ID.

It is difficult to associate ID approaches with a 'Bildung-Didactic' human image. For a Bildung-Didactic, didactic models can be used that stand in the bourgeois tradition of humanistic didactics and enlightenment. In Europe, and above all in the German-speaking world, the thematization of didactics is tied to Enlightenment pedagogy. Wolfgang Ratke originally used the term *didacta* to describe the qualification of teachers. Enlightenment pedagogy distinguishes the strong accentuation of the capability of reason. As critical citizens, people should give themselves reasonable laws instead of being governed by church and king. In order to uncover the potential of reason, adolescents should practice independent thinking and judgment. If in the following, we talk about (educational) didactics, this is in the tradition of enlightenment pedagogy and humanistic didactics. Bildung-Didactics stands in the tradition of bourgeois epistemology and bourgeois didactics. This tradition and continuity are reflected in the transfer of the educational characteristics of power and freedom into the empirically founded concepts of explorative curiosity and self-efficacy.

The identification of explorative curiosity and perceived self-efficacy as empirical characteristics of Bildung bears consequences for a Bildung-oriented didactic. For a Bildung-oriented didactization of teaching and learning scenarios, the challenge is to design controllable learning situations or learning spaces that challenge curiosity of the learner, and at the same time offer solvable tasks to ensure the development of perceived self-efficacy. The aim of a Bildung-oriented didactic is to spare learners the repeated experience of overstraining and failure as well as the lack of learning impulses for their explorative curiosity.

The following checklist is based on the dimensions of

- self-efficacy experiences,
- explorative curiosity,
- dialogical exchange, and
- the structuring of the learning space.

These dimensions result from the positions developed on Bildung (cf. Kergel, 2018, 2019). The merge of these dimensions can lead to a Bildungsraum (educational space, or Bildung – Space). The checklist has a double perspective:

- It can be read as a list of criteria when developing teaching and learning scenarios in the sense of a Bildung-oriented didactics.
- The criteria can also be used for an evaluation. From this perspective, the criteria become quality characteristics. The quality of the teaching/ learning process can be assessed according to the extent to which the criteria could be fulfilled (cf. Kergel, 2018).

In summary, the dimensions can be understood as the factors or didactic framework in which a Bildung spaces can unfold.

Dimension 1: Bildung-Characteristic perceived self-efficacy

- Do the given learning challenges and tasks allow a differentiation of complexity? Through such differentiation the learner can deal with the learning challenge/task according to the individual competence level of the learner.
- Is a participative, or action and production-oriented learning made possible? An action and production-oriented learning enables the learner to experience herself as self-sufficient.
- Do clear, transparent structures that guide the learning process exist? Along these transparent structures, the subject can develop his learning beyond external authoritarian influences.

Dimension 2: Bildung-Characteristic *explorative curiosity*

- Can learners contribute their intrinsic interest in knowledge to the design and structure of the learning challenge?
- Does a participative, or action and production-oriented learning specifically involves the intrinsic curiosity of the learners?

Dimension 3: Dialogical interaction

- Are opportunities given for dialogical interaction?
- Is there a dialogical, appreciative communication atmosphere and/or exit rules for dialogue?
- Is there positive reinforcement of the learning performance and the willingness to try?

Dimension 4: Structure of the learning space

- Which interaction opportunities (e.g., group tables, retreat possibilities, a digital learning space) are given by the spatial infrastructure?
- Does the learning challenge/task provide authentic learning situations?
- Can learners adjust the given tasks according to their preferred learning style?

The criteria listed can be applied to the design of Bildung-based teaching/learning scenarios. In addition, this teaching/learning scenario can be evaluated by comparing the criteria formulated in the didactic framework model with its concrete didactic strategies. The concrete teaching/learning scenario can be examined to see whether it can be assigned to the didactic structure, according to Bildung-oriented didactics:

- Why is the present teaching/learning scenario a Bildung-oriented teaching/learning scenario (or not)?
- In order to take the temporal course of teaching/learning processes into account in didactic planning, a course plan can be drawn up in addition to the criteria. This process planning can be oriented to the following key questions:
- When and why is each task set?
- How are these questions dealt with? Why, and in what time frame?
- How are the work results secured?

Notes

1 The term subjectivation refers to the inscription of social hierarchies and dependencies in the individual's relationship to himself and the world. From this perspective, subjectivation forms the analytical counter-concept to Bildung. Instead of constructing a positively connoted self/world relationship based on explorative curiosity and expectations of self-efficacy, the subject is formed by prefigured societal hierarchies and role models which precede the individual. Subjectivation can be contrasted with Bildung. Subjectivation is a process in which the individual is integrated into the social hierarchies. In social reality, moments of Bildung and subjectivation merge into one another so that they cannot be differentiated as sharply as they are in the conceptual sphere, which define 'Bildung' as becoming a self-determined subject rather than 'subjectivation.'

2 One reason to think about learning with the model of learning theories is the diversity of meaning of the term learning. Learning theories are models and hypotheses used to describe and explain learning processes psychologically. The complex process of learning is explained with principles and rules that are as simple as possible (cf. Schaller, 2012). From a genealogical perspective, learning theories are a result of the establishment of (pedagogical) psychology as a science, which increasingly developed and established itself from the 1840s onwards.

3 The Boston Massacre was an incident during the American Revolution in British North America on 5 March 1770, in which British troops killed five civilians.

The event, called a "massacre" for propaganda purposes, became a beacon for the groups pursuing colonial independence and contributed to the outbreak of the American War of Independence.

4 As an epoch of philosophy, German idealism developed in the 40 years between the publication of Kant's main epistemological work *Die Kritik der reinen Vernunft* (the Critique of Pure Reason, 1781) and Hegel's death in 1831. The starting point was Kant's epistemological understanding of the human being as a rational being: The use of reason enables the individual to recognize the world without God or other instances of knowledge on the other side.

5 'Individual' describes the single human being. The subject, in turn, can be described as the dimension of the individual's experience in which the individual developed a self/world relationship. The individual is not only 'there' (e.g., like a stone), but it experiences that it is 'there.' It experiences itself as a feeling being in the world or its 'being there.'

6 Writing enhances and fosters abstract thinking, which finds its manifestation in the epistemology of German idealism. The 'I' as an epistemological premise of German idealism constitutes itself via reading and writing.

7 This dominance of visual culture appears on television as the leading medium of the electronic age and is slowly being replaced by the multimedia nature of the digital age.

8 Bourgeois writing is first and foremost a realistic writing. From this point of view Realism as a literary epoch is inherently a bourgeois kind of literature (cf. Lukács, 1971).

9 It is probably the most famous early encyclopedia in today's understanding and originated under the editorship of Denis Diderot and Jean Baptiste le Rond d'Alembert. The encyclopedia contains contributions by 142 editors, the encyclopedists. The first volume appeared in 1751. In 1780 the series was completed with the 35th and last volume. The Encyclopédie is one of the main works of the Enlightenment. It contains more than 70,000 articles.

10 Armchair ethnography is a form of ethnological research in which the knowledge of other cultures was reconstructed from travelogues by merchants, missionaries, or colonizers. It gained its name because this form of ethnological research is carried out from the desk.

11 The German translation of the term 'formation of public opinion' refers explicitly to the concept of 'Bildung': Meinungsbildung (Bildung of an opinion).

12 In times of war newspapers were used for propaganda purposes. In some places, such as Russia, this led to a controlled newspaper sector and public sphere (cf. Bösch, 2019, p. 96).

13 http://www.columbia.edu/acis/ets/CCREAD/etscc/kant.html. Last accessed: 3 March 2020.

14 http://www.columbia.edu/acis/ets/CCREAD/etscc/kant.html. Last accessed: 3 March 2020.

15 http://www.columbia.edu/acis/ets/CCREAD/etscc/kant.html. Last accessed: 3 March 2020.

16 From an epistemological perspective, it should be mentioned that Bildung is not an anthropological constant but a concept which is part of the discourses of civil society. The concept of Bildung was developed in the circle of European culture and therefore represents a Eurocentric perspective on the development processes of individuals.

17 Wolfgang Ratke (1571–1631) originally used the term didacta to describe the qualification of teachers.

Chapter 3

Linear learning in the book culture

One can refer to the terms Erziehung and Bildung as heuristic concepts. These concepts can be used to analyze the development of education and the 'motion of learning' in civil society. In its beginning teaching and learning were embedded in an authoritarian relationship and thus more Erziehung-oriented. In the 17th century, the basic conviction about the essence of teaching and learning was that the pupil learns what the teacher teaches. This teaching and learning culture can be analyzed as an Erziehung-Culture. This Erziehung-Culture possessed tradition beyond civil society. In the tradition of medieval pedagogy, elementary instruction was held in monastic and secular schools. The pupils had to learn what was taught.

Reading aloud or dictating and rewriting at universities also followed this logic until the 19th century. Nevertheless, the power of knowledge changed: the foundations of universities in Prague (1348), Vienna (1365), and Heidelberg (1386) prepared the hegemonic cultural claim in the field of knowledge of civil society. Until today universities presented the centers of knowledge, and these centers were located in cities. The cities became the centers of civil culture and power. The motion of learning developed in the course of the transformation processes of civil society. Based on the analysis of the media epochs of bourgeois society, the movement of learning can be reconstructed and presented genealogically. The starting point is an analysis heuristic based on an entanglement between media and the motion of learning. Learning and the media and socio-cultural development of learning is an effect of bourgeois society's transformation processes. If this socio-cultural dimension of (civic) learning is not adequately analyzed and considered, it will be difficult to develop sound strategies for teaching and learning in the digital age.

3.1 Comenius and the beginning of the pedagogical book culture

In the late 18th century, the efficacy of authoritarian teaching and learning was increasingly questioned – at least on a theoretical level. The learning subject and their self-determination were increasingly the focus of pedagogical considerations. This new understanding of learning was strongly influenced by John Amos Comenius, who developed the first picture book for children. Comenius developed a sustained influence on teaching and learning which is still noticeable today (cf. Kergel, 2020). A key basic premise is to teach everything comprehensively – "omnes omnia omnino." One innovative approach was that education should apply to all people. "All" meant every single person regardless of age, property, social status, and gender.

Already during his lifetime Comenius enjoyed great prestige as a scholar and as a consultant for school development. His written works are of longer duration. His main educational work is the *Didactica Magna* (*Great Teaching*), one of the most important writings in the history of didactics. In the book Comenius unfolds a pedagogical system which already contains all the essential principles, categories, and basic questions that move modern pedagogy: from basic anthropological questions to educational goals, from learning content and methodological questions to questions of school organization. Also known is Comenius' book *Orbis sensualium pictus* (*The Visible World in Pictures*), one of Goethe's favourite books. It is an illustrated Latin-German language book for children. *Orbis Sensualium Pictus* is regarded as the first modern picture book for children and a precursor of today's textbooks. As the subtitle indicates, the whole world of things and life should be painted and named. Until the 19th century, *Orbis Sensualium Pictus* became a model for similar works that wanted to familiarize children with the real world. The literature for children increasingly established itself.

Comenius anticipated the meaning of the book for bourgeois educational theory and practice as the anthropological premise that everybody can and should learn – regardless of social background and status.

Both of these aspects – the book as an educational tool and the learning human being as anthropological constant – are features of a 'new understanding' of learning. This new understanding of learning was developed by progressive educators in the group of philanthropists such as Joachim Heinrich Campe or Peter Villaume. The new understanding of learning was based on the fostering of curiosity, encouragement, self-activity, and confidence in success. This approach partly anticipated Humboldt's Bildung–Concept and grew from the bourgeois concept of the active human being.

3.2 From 'ascension through education' to 'the birth of reading in public schools'

In its beginning children's literature had a religious orientation, followed by a bourgeois moral orientation. From the middle of the 19th century onwards, pure fantasy and adventure stories were increasingly accepted as children's literature.

The new understanding of teaching and learning was deeply linked with the bourgeois book culture, as can be seen in the example of Heinrich

Campe. Heinrich Campe was one of the most important German enlightenment educators and philanthropists, who founded his educational institute in
1777. Campe is also considered one of the inventors of children's and young
adult literature. He published educational books that were intended to educationally influence adolescents in the sense of enlightenment pedagogy. Since
this time, books and learning have been inextricably linked with each other.
Educators like Campe wrote children's literature and philosophers like Rousseau wrote novels on child-raising. Books became an important educational
medium – with sometimes peculiar results. Johann Heinrich Pestalozzi of
Switzerland (1746–1827), another well-known representative of enlightenment education, was strongly influenced by Rousseau. Pestalozzi wanted to
educate his son Jakob according to Rousseau's ideas. Pestalozzi did not reflect
the hypothetical literary character of Rousseau's 'Émile.' He understood the
book as a concrete educational manual, and put his son under pressure to cor-
respond literally to the ideal image by an education à la Rousseau. Pestalozzi's
educational experiment failed dramatically. Jakob was unable to write even
at the age of 11 and suffered emotionally from the consequences of education
until his death at the age of 32. Nevertheless, Pestalozzi continued to deal
with the possibilities of education in theory and practice.

Civil society is a society of education. Educators like Campe use the book
as an educational medium. At the same time, Campe also criticized the negative effects of reading or 'false reading.' He criticized the way increasing
literacy and the expansion of the book market changed the social structure of
the reading public. Women and young people formed new groups of readers,
and the success of popular literature, mostly translated from French, changed
the book market. Moreover, a new German literature arose in the tradition
of Empfindsamkeit. In consequence, new forms of reading emerged, characterized by a passionate and emotionally identifiable attitude to its reception.
This transformation of the book culture led to a new discussion about the
pedagogical meaning of reading. The Lesewut (German for *reading craze*) or
the Lesesucht (*reading mania*) are terms critics used, interpreting this transformation of the market as a danger to the rational social order of civil society.
According to these discussions, the main 'risk groups' were young people
and women. By their arguments, adult men were less likely to be affected as
they devoted themselves primarily to non-fiction rather than to fiction that
stimulated the imagination.

In addition to the link between book culture and bourgeois education, the
new understanding of learning led to a new understanding of intergenera-
tional relations. In the early civil society, childhood and youth were regarded
as fully fledged phases of life. This approach changed with a new understanding of learning. Childhood and youth were considered as phases of development in which the foundation is laid for social advancement – school and
universities opened up the possibility to become part of the functional elites
and thus be a part of either privileged civil service or the liberal academic

professions. Until our times, this bourgeois understanding of 'ascension through education' was one of the central topoi of the self-understanding discourses on civil society and the role of education within civil society. Ascension through education applies to everyone and replaces the 'inheritance law' of feudal society. According to this paradigm, everyone has the chance and the task to 'find his/her future place within society.' To do so, everyone must strive after learning for success. According to this conception of education it was (is) necessary that everybody should learn – at least to read and write. In consequence, public schools were established.

The discourse on teaching and learning in civil society saw its impact in the public school system. One example is Prussia and its leading role in this process. In Prussia, Wilhelm von Humboldt was a strong supporter of the elementary school. The elementary school was no longer the school for poor people but rather the first link in the education chain for all school-age children, comparable to today's primary school. Grammar schools were established, as well as secondary schools that prepared for civil service or university attendance. A compulsory curriculum was introduced in 1837. The nationalization of the school system and educational reforms were accompanied by general compulsory education. In Prussia this was established in 1717, while in Great Britain the public educational system did not exist until 1830s. Although compulsory school attendance regulations had already existed for many years, it was not until the 19th century that it was possible to enforce the actual general attendance of children at school. In the 19th century, the elementary school expanded. Nearly all classes learned reading and writing at least on a basal level, the core competencies of book culture.

The emergence of the public school in civil society can be considered a representation of book culture in the pedagogical field. It was only with book culture that reading and writing became basic 'cultural techniques' for the general population. Until far into modern times most people were illiterate, so the question of reading books, especially for children and young people, did not arise. The invention of printing in the mid-15th century made it easier for children and young people to access literature – albeit only to a limited extent at first. Nevertheless, print products and literature for children became increasingly established.

In the book culture of bourgeois society, the question of education was closely connected with raising children. Until today the individual's entry into the school meant an inauguration into the sphere of reading and writing. The 'seriousness of life' represented in the requirement to perform started with entry into school and confrontation of the grading system. Before this entry learning was mainly an audio-visually experience; in school, learning became training in abstract practice. The immediacy of audio-visually experienced learning is replaced by deciphering and producing letters. The meaning of reading and writing can also be shown through the activities of important persons who shaped the new understanding of education.

3.3 From the inconsequent realization of ideal equality to the counterpublic

Public schools had and still have the task to create favorable learning conditions for all children through an enlightened pedagogy. But one has to be aware that this egalitarian approach had its limitations: At the beginning, the social advancement through education applied to boys. Girls from the middle classes were also included in the pedagogical considerations – as future mothers and educators. As this example shows, the history of civil society is also a history of inherent contradictions: The concept of equality has its limitations, *inter alia*, in the question of gender/sexual equality and social justice. These inherent contradictions have been urgent questions up to today. The media manifestation of the inherent contradictions is the emergence of counter-discourse. Counter-discourse is a peripheral part of the public sphere. The civil public presupposes that every citizen has the opportunity to raise his voice, to listen to it, and to be included in the discourse. Accordingly, 'participation is the real foundation of democracy' (cf. Wimmer, 2018, p. 248). However, there is always the risk that not all voices are heard and that some citizens or entire marginalized groups 'have no voice.' Spivak (2008) summarizes the (cultural) voicelessness of marginalized groups/individuals with the concept of subalternity. Others speak *for* or *about* subalterns so that subalterns do not have their voice in civil society's of hegemonic narratives.

With hegemonic narratives, hegemonic discourses are established. With reference to Gramsci, one can also speak of 'cultural hegemony' (cf. Gramsci, 1982). The concept of cultural hegemony encompasses the induction and consent of the ruled. Cultural hegemony can be understood as a form of ideological dominance that is reproduced in the media.

The media also communicates the establishment of hierarchies and dependency relationships. Bourgeois guiding ideas and virtues such as diligence, competition principle, and (self-) optimization are articulated in the media (cf. Kergel, 2020). Individuals and marginalized groups who are not compatible with the dominant guiding ideas are in turn excluded or portrayed as deficient. These excluded groups are either not depicted or are depicted in a discriminating manner. Fraser (1992) makes this clear in a critique of Habermas:

Women of all classes and ethnicities were excluded from official political participation on the basis of gender status, while plebeian men were formally excluded by property qualifications. Moreover, in many cases women and men of racialized ethnicities of all classes were excluded on racial grounds (Fraser, 1992, p. 118).

This is where the struggle for subaltern counterpublicity begins

I propose to call these subaltern counterpublics in order to signal that they are parallel discursive arenas where members of subordinated social groups invent and circulate counterdiscourses to formulate oppositional interpretations of their identities, interests, and needs.

(Fraser, 1992, S.122)

The dialectic interplay between the mainstream discourse and the subversive counter-discourse is one factor of the development of the public sphere. The history of book culture in the Gutenberg Galaxy provides many examples of this. At the same time, it can also be seen how slowly (some) positions from the counter-discourse gradually become part of the mainstream discourse in the course of a social, discursive self-enlightenment. The counter-discourse is the counterpart to the mainstream, which enables learning in society as a whole at the level of the public sphere.

3.4 About the Vormärz (Pre-March) or counterpublic: an example

In civil society, the formation of counterpublicity is bound to changes in media. In the book culture of the Gutenberg Galaxy, the counter-discourse was formed through leaflets, newspapers, and books. In Germany, "Vormärz" (Pre-March) represents a literary epoch that can be understood as an epoch of the counterpublic and "counter-publication." In the period between 1815 (the end of the so-called "Wars of liberation" against Napoleon) and the beginning of the March Revolution in 1848, a literary milieu emerged in Germany in which writers were able to establish themselves as independent authors and journalists. The innovations in the printing technology and the growing reading public, as well as publishing houses, enabled writers to need neither a princely patron nor any "bread and butter" profession. Writers such as Gutzkow and Laube, who became known as Junges Deutschland (Young Germany), rejected dogmatism and advocated values ranging from individualism and freedom of expression to socialist ideals. Representatives of Young Germany, to which the poet Heine also partly belongs, had to flee into exile. The main reason was the political orientation of the publications; the publications of Pre-March's Young Germans were oriented towards bourgeois and even socialist emancipation and they were not tolerated by the authorities.

3.5 The counterpublic as part of a societal Bildung-process

In the course of the transformations of bourgeois society and in the context of media change, new forms of bourgeois and anti-bourgeois culture emerged all the time. The counterpublic is sometimes exposed to repression, as can be seen from the exile of Young Germany. It is not surprising that anonymity from the earliest days of bourgeois society up to our time is a characteristic of counterpublicity. In 1793, for example, the philosopher Fichte anonymously published the leaflet "Zurückforderung der Denkfreiheit von den Fürsten

Europeans, die sie bisher Unterdrückten. Eine Rede" ("Revindication of the Freedom of Thoughts from Europe's Rulers who Suppressed it Until Now"). This work by Fichte was prompted by his experiences with the Prussian censorship authority and is a fierce defense of freedom of thought (cf. Kühn, 2012, p. 156). Later Fichte lost his professorship in Jena because he was accused of atheism, but unofficially his sympathy for the French revolution and Fichte's 'Jacobinism' should be the true reason (cf. Kühn, 2012).

Positions which are directed against the cultural hegemony, the discursive mainstream, and the ruling power bear the danger of exclusion. This is not surprising since the counterpublic constantly challenges the dominant opinions and the silent consensus of the public. Despite this – or precisely because of this – the counter-discourse and counterpublic established itself in the beourgeois society's media landscape as an indispensable counterpart to the cultural hegemony. Recently this has become evident in Wikileaks and Anonymous. From a Bildung-oriented point of view, the counterpublic is indispensable to the public sphere. Within Bildung-Theory, learning is the performative extension of knowledge. It requires people to raise voices which are not yet heard. Thus, the societal knowledge can be extended. In consequence subaltern actors participate in the discourse, and society has the chance to adjust policy and change social practice to the needs of this group. In other word, the counterpublic is the dissent and the objection which ensures that the process of self-enlightenment and therefore self-education does not stop. On the level of a society which is obliged to the value setting of Bildung the counterpublic, the objection, is needed. A society that bans the contradiction and the counterpublic is a society that puts limitations of the potential of Bildung-based self-enlightenment and stops the motion of learning, which always need new impulses to generate new knowledge.

3.6 From half-Bildung to nationalism – side-effects of the Gutenberg Galaxy

One can conclude that on a media level, in civil society, education is strongly linked to reading and writing and to book culture in general. From an Erziehung-oriented point of view, printed books provide objective knowledge about the world. The book is the metonymic manifestation of the teacher and the reader of the learner (Zu-Erziehenden). Through Erziehung the learner becomes a part of civil society's symbolic order.

Bildung, in turn, stresses the self-activity of the bourgeois subject. In reading and writing, in engaging *in* and *with* the world, the individual unfolds itself.

Besides this discourse on education, the book culture of the Gutenberg Galaxy carried a tangible impact: the literacy rate increased. Reading and writing became core competencies which should be taught and learned in school. The picture books and literature for childhood and youth were established. Education established itself as a central feature of civil society. But with the economic, media, and socio-cultural changes in civil society, the educational discourse and policy also changed. The Prussian school system reproduced social inequality at the level of education and the concept of Bildung lost its emancipative implications[1]. In 1903, in a chapter of the *Encyclopaedic Handbook of Pedagogy*, Friedrich Paulsen speaks of 'Half-Bildung' (Halbbildung).

> The opposition between *Bildung and Halbbildung(semi-* or superficial education) or *Unbildung* (lack of education) is not primarily a social but a self-critical definition that actually constitutes the concept of *Bildung*. That *Bildung* cannot be restricted to a known content; that the danger of *Oberbildung* (overeducation) or *Verbildung* (miseducation) would lurk here; that the form oflmowledge is more important than knowledge itself.
> (Koselleck, 2002, p. 190, emphasis in original)

Adorno later took up the notion Half-Bildung and problematized it. According to Paulsen, the higher education system mediated knowledge about culture. But in this process the emancipative 'kernel' of Bildung got lost. To describe the loss of the culture's emancipative implications, the term Half-Bildung has been established. Half-Bildung is to be understood as superficial Bildung. This Bildung is shallow because it deals with typical Bildung-Objects such as painting, music, and poetry. The examination of these Bildung-Objects, however, does not serve the self-development of the subject and the unfolding of his power and freedom. Instead, Half-Bildung is used as a strategy to gain respect as an educated and cultivated human being. Accordingly, Half-Bildung becomes 'cultural capital' to gain a good position in society (cf. Bourdieu, 2001). As Half-Bildung, Bildung turns into a commodity. Bildung can be purchased, for example, in the form of paintings and piano lessons. The cultural citizen distinguishes himself from other citizens. Knowledge about Bildung objects is a symbol for the belonging to an elitist circle. In this sense, Half-Bildung means the application of domination knowledge, which excludes other – often poor – people (cf. Bourdieu, 2001). (Half-)Bildung requires a skillful use of language (thus the author is always in the possession of Bildung).

The appreciation of language can be analyzed as an effect of book culture. In other words, an effect of the Gutenberg Galaxy's book culture is the centralization of language. This centralization of language led to the concept of a cultural entity that was represented by a common language and the concept of the "cultural bation" (cf. Herder, 2004). According to Herder, language is the ontological gap between cultures. The geographical frame of cultures are nations. This connection between nationalism and the bourgeois culture manifests in the names of journals. Newspapers were called *Gazette of the United States* or *National Gazette*, or in Germany *Journal von und für Deutschland*

(*Journal of and for Germany*) or *Teutsche Merkur* (*German Mercury*). Reading and writing became cultural techniques that contributed in the long run to cultural identity – a 'folk' possesses a 'mother.' A spatial expansion accompanied the book culture of bourgeois society. This spatial development was also part of the technological and media developments of capitalism and led from the Gutenberg Galaxy to the Electronic Age. These technological, media, and cultural developments also set learning in motion again.

Note

1 In Germany exists until now a structured school system in which pupils at lower secondary level attend different types of school. These different types of schools prepare students for different roles in society. Social hierarchies appear metonymically in different types of schools.

Chapter 4

Informal-accidental learning in the electronic age

4.1 The becoming of the electronic age

Industrialization led from book culture to the electronic age. The industrialization's country of origin was England. In the 18th century, technical innovations such as the steam engine made it possible to produce goods by machine and thus achieve a new form of economic growth. Most European countries were affected by the process of industrialization between the middle of the 19th century and the outbreak of the First World War in 1914.

4.1.1 The Victorian Internet[1]

Technical innovations gave mass media a further upswing. The literacy of broad parts of the population provided a base which the newspaper market developed into a mass market. Six-figure circulations reached almost the million mark. Newspapers were mainly sold in cities. The booming newspaper market was an expression of progressive urbanization. Magazines strengthened urban centrality as the newspapers strengthened national identity before. The city became a metropolis and was presented *in* and *via* the press. As another technical innovation, the telegraph led to an increased progress of globalization. With telegraphy, the exchange of information became faster. Newspapers such as the 1855-founded *Daily Telegraph* took advantage of this as a business model. This business model was the result of a 'cabling of the world' – which is continued today with the Internet. Standage analyzed telegraphy as the Victorian Internet. The origins of telegraphy date back to the 1830s. In the 1850s, the cabling of the world began. Despite massive costs and setbacks this cabling drove forward. In 1851 there was a connection between London and Paris. In 1855 the connection reached up to Crimea and in 1866 the connection was across the Atlantic. From the 1870s, telegraph cables from Europe reached Australia and Beijing. As with the printing press, the spread of the new technology led to standardization. Since 1865 Morse code was the standard language of telegraphy.

The telegraph strengthened the position of the metropolis, as it connected (European) metropolises with each other. This new technology became a factor of power. Like the press, political powers tried to control telegraphy. In Germany, for example, telegraphy was put under the control of the post office. The cable networks served as an information advantage for businesses and the first news agencies were founded at this time. In short, telegraphy brought the world together and bourgeois media modernity began.

4.1.2 From the new sound of modern urbanity to the objective gaze of new media

In addition to the establishment of telegraphy, the auditive dimension also augmented perceptions of the world and reality. In 1876, Alexander Graham Bell patented the telephone in the USA. It was initially established as a medium for urban agglomerations (cf. Hartmann, 2006, p. 101). The first users of the telephone were mainly functional elites such as bankers and brokers as well as doctors and lawyers (cf. Hartmann, 2006, p. 103). The establishment of private and broad use of the telephone did not take place until the 1960s and 1970s. Nevertheless, in the early days of the bourgeois media modernity, the telephone created an auditory linkage of the world. Another auditive change was the gramophone and the record industry.

Around 1900 the commercial sale of gramophones had started. In the USA in particular, the recorded music market developed into a booming industry with sales well over 100 million dollars in the pre-war period. Sales slumped after the First World War. This slump was mainly due to the effect of the radios and later to the global economic crisis (cf. Hörisch, 2004, p. 267). Sales in the USA fell to a record low of six million dollars in 1933 (Hörisch, 2004, p. 267). From the perspective of media theory, it can be said that the gramophone was used to 'rearrange time and space'. What was new about the phonograph and the gramophone was the way they transformed fleeting sounds into a material. The sound became lasting and left a reproducible trace. At the same time, this meant that sound in technical reproduction lost its connection to its origin. The apparatus separated the spoken word from the speaker's body, the music from the instrument, and the rattling of hooves from the horses. With this detachment of sound from its origin, the technical reproduction of sound was attributed with the fact that 'time can be overcome towards the future'. Sounds of past times become audible again. But also the urban 'sound of the big city' could be recorded.

Since the 1880s there has been interplay between media change and social transformation. New electronic transmission media such as telegraphy and telephone provided a new form of media reality. This auditory dimension had been complemented by the extension of a visual dimension. While photography and the daguerreotype saw the light of day in 1838, the development of various film cameras fell into the 1890s. With photography and film, a new type of world perception has been created. The world was not portrayed by objects such as writers or painters but was supposedly realistically reproduced via technical media. The birth of film solved a problem that could not be solved with the mere human eye – the starting point was the question of whether a galloping horse has all its legs in the air at once or not. This lasting and controversial question was solved with twelve cameras and later 24. The cameras were installed at short intervals from each other. In 1978, Eadweard Muybridge took a series of shots with these cameras. At the end, this experiment provided two different insights. First, the horse left the ground with all four legs while galloping. Also, the medium of knowledge was the objective camera and not the human being with his subjective perspective. The supposedly objective representation of reality through the new medium of pictures in motion had a highly suggestive effect on the individuum. Instead of objectively depicting reality, the moving images created a new reality.

4.1.3 The ideological impact of pictures in motion

With the emergence of film, globalization was driven forward with a Western Imperial impact. For example, 50 movies *about* Japan were shown for Germany until 1911. These movies were mainly French productions, which at that time had the supremacy over movie production. By contrast, only one film *from* Japan was shown in Germany until 1911 (cf. Bösch, 2019, p. 144).

The first crisis in the film industry in 1906 led to the restructuring of commercial film and the film industry in 1910. Initially, film was a carnival attraction that attracted the lower classes. Now cinema became more bourgeois. A narrative cinema found its way into film halls. These film halls were built especially for the 'narrative movie.' One example of such is the film *The Birth of a Nation*.

D.W. Griffith's 1915 film *The Birth of a Nation* was a sympathetic representation of the Ku Klux Klan and was very popular for American audiences. President Woodrow Wilson arranged a private screening of the film at the White House. D.W. Griffith's controversial film about the Civil War and Reconstruction showed the Ku Klux Klan as the courageous savior of a post-war South, devastated by northern swindlers and immoral blacks: "The Birth of a Nation depicted America's providential passage from war to peace in its final climactic scenes. It showed Black soldiers pillaging and threatening White southerners during Reconstruction" (Ambrosius, 2007, p. 36, emphasis in original).

The film was an immediate blockbuster and led to a revival of the KKK. Until the film, the Ku Klux Klan, founded in 1865 by Confederate veterans in Pulaski, Tennessee, was a regional organization. At the time the film was released, the KKK had almost entirely disappeared. The racist Jim Crow narrative of *The Birth of a Nation*, coupled with America's unfolding anti–immigrant climate, made the film a recruitment tool for the KKK. The success story of this film is also a story of media change. The movie *The Birth of a Nation* was based on a novel by Thomas Dixon Jr. (*The Clansman*).[2]

The success of this narration unfolded with the film and not with the book. "Dixon wanted the United States to enter the war against Imperial Germany earlier than Wilson did. The phenomenal box office success of The Birth of a Nation convinced him of Hollywood's power to shape public opinion" (Ambrosius, 2007, para. 36).

As medium the film also raised educational concerns about the harmful effects of the new medium. At the same time, the educational potential of the film was also discussed. In Germany, this led to the founding of the Institute of Official Counseling and Inspection of Films for teaching purposes (cf. Hüther, 2017, p. 22).

4.1.4 The urban metropolis – home of the masses

Around 1900, innovations in the media became more concentrated and the world increasingly turned into a global village. The word 'television' was first introduced in 1900 at the Paris World Exposition. One can speak of a media revolution in 1900. In 1900 Zeppelin managed to steer his airship with engine and rudder. The year 1900 was an important year of a development that led man to the moon and in 1904 the first airplane took off from the ground. In 1909 the first flight over the English Channel took place, and in 1919 the first flight over the Atlantic. In 1969 the first man landed on the moon.

From 1900 onwards the basic media of the electronic age developed. In addition to the telephone film became popular, accompanied by the spread of the gramophone and cameras for the public. Finally, telegraphy developed into radio in the 1920s. Around 1900 the commercial sale of gramophones started.

The new media culture was embedded in a mass culture which contained department stores, sports events, zoos, and finally cinemas (in 1912, 1500 stable cinemas existed in Germany, cf. Hüther, 2015, p. 19). This culture for the masses was situated in the metropolis, habitat of the 'masses.' The mass media culture, which developed through telegraphy, cinema, and radio, corresponds to a concentration of the masses in cities.

The 19th century was an era of intense urbanization. In 1800 there lived about one billion people, in 1930, this already increased to two billion (cf. Koselleck, 2000, p. 13). The world population was increasingly located within the cities. The 19th and 20th centuries were a time of intensive urbanization. No previous epoch has experienced such a spatial compression of social life. Existence and living in the metropolis became an economically and culturally dominant form of life. London grew from 900,000 inhabitants to 7.3 million between 1800 and 1913. People came to the metropolis in search of work and prosperity.

The urban infrastructure was not prepared for this massive influx of people. This led to hygiene problems and social conflicts. At the same time, emancipatory movements such as the women's and labor movements in the cities were formed – strikes became part of modern urban life.

4.1.5 The media ecology of the urban metropolis

In view of an almost infinite mass of houses, travel documents and literary figures created the image of the 'sea of houses.' Many felt that man in the big city appeared to be torn away like a 'drop in the ocean' in the stream of masses (cf. Payer, 2017, p. 36). Industrialization finally turned cities into economic centers. The urban–modern city and the industrial system presuppose each other. The industrial revolution broke into urban space with the railway. While the factories mostly settled on the outskirts of cities the railway lines crossed the urban environment for each inhabitant to perceive concretely.

With all these social transformations a new urban media ecology emerged. The rapid social, technical, and economic changes brought a flood of new sounds that many had yet to adapt. "The psychological basis of the metropolitan type of individuality consist in the intensification of nervous stimulation which results from the swift and uninterrupted change of outer and inner stimuli" (Simmel, 1969, p. 48, emphasis in original).

The new sounds led to the 'Bruitism' movement; sounds were taken from urban extra-musical sources and implemented in music pieces. With the expansion of the cities, it became necessary to link the countryside more closely to the center. The horse tram initially established itself as an efficient and cheap means of mass transport. At the turn of the century, the horse tram was finally replaced by the electrified tram. The use of electrical energy to drive rail-bound vehicles meant a revolution in inner-city traffic. Light wagons with large, effortlessly controlled driving forces resulted in an enormous increase in capacity and speed. The new media ecology led to a sensory overload and permanent attacks on all senses.

> With each crossing of the street, with the tempo and multiplicity of economic, occupational, and social life, the city sets up a deep contrast with small town and rural life with reference to the sensory foundations of psychic life. The metropolis exacts from man as a discriminating creature a different amount of consciousness than does rural life.
>
> (Simmel, 1969, p. 48)

It was no coincidence that the number of specialists for nervous disorders increased rapidly at this time. The constantly changing impressions and stimuli, as well as the increasing streams of information, were sometimes difficult to cope with (cf. Payer, 2017, p. 40). The romantic image of the city resting at night was replaced by the insomnia of the metropolises. This was also reflected in new auditive experiences. Thus, there was "talk of the 'surf of the big city,' of a 'clearly audible roar and noise,' a roar that gives the impression of a continuous, diffuse, seemingly unstoppable back and forth waving background noise" (Payer, 2017, p. 36, translation David Kergel).

The electric trams traversed metropolises like Berlin and reflected an urban restlessness. This restlessness is an urban restlessness of the masses. The term masses increasingly received a negative connotation. Among other ways the bourgeoisie separated itself from the masses via Half-Bildung. Culture in a civil society became an urban mass culture. This urban mass culture stood in contrast to the serious culture of the bourgeois. In particular, radio became a mass medium in the 1920s.

In the first half of the 1920s, radio stations increasingly emerged. Instead of producing a product that satisfies a need, the early radio manufacturers founded radio stations to create demand for their devices.[3] In some Western countries such as Germany, radio initially remained under state control. This state control was also intended to prevent communists from broadcasting radical political content, especially in times of revolutionary movements at the beginning of the 1920s.

In summary, it can be said that mass culture developed in the cities from 1900 onwards. This new mass culture limited the literary dominance of the book culture. In addition to written language, moving images and auditive media also emerged. This media transformation laid the (mass-)cultural foundation for the electronic age, which was only replaced by the digital age almost 100 years later.

4.1.6 Modernity and revolution – towards ever-changing concepts

The urban metropolis is deeply connected with the concept of modernity. The concept of modernity is one of the most dazzling and open-ended concepts of the social sciences. Therefore, a sharpening of the used understanding of modernity seems inevitable. In the following passages, from a historicizing, sociological perspective, 'modernity' is defined as the self-understanding discourse of civil society.

In principle, the term 'modern' distinguishes itself from something old and thus is a term that marks a transition. In civil society, modern is the secular, industrialized civil society that unfolds in urban mass culture.

The self-thematization of a modern society is based more or less explicitly on the intertwining of economic, media, and socio-cultural change. This complex change, which is marked by the term modernity, is often associated with the awareness of a crisis (cf. Kergel, 2020). The old social formation becomes fractured and finally is replaced by the 'modern' social formation. Modern society views itself as a more complex social formation and thus distinguishes itself from the previous 'old' social formation. This old and now-fractured social formation is assumed to be less complex. The bourgeois idea of progress and the concept of revolution continue to have an effect in determining the modern. In other words, modernity is a bourgeois term such as the term 'revolution' in the meaning of a deeply radical change towards something new. As a term for social/

cultural transformation which departs from the 'old,' the notion 'modern/ modernity' bears marks of a revolutionary process. The French Revolution shaped the concept of radical change, which continues to develop the term 'revolution' until the present day. Originally the term 'revolution' came from astronomy and described the movement of the planets in their orbit. The movement led the planets back to their starting point. Within the political discourse, the term 're-volvere' refers to the return to an earlier state. With civil society, the notion of revolution received a new meaning. The radical social transformation in the course of the French revolution has given rise to the modern idea of a revolution as a radical socio-cultural change (cf. Gerber, 2018, p. 85).

> The invention of the printing press; the spread of literacy and reading; the inventions of the compass, telescope, and microscope; the development of the experimental sciences; the discovery of the globe; overseas colonization and the comparison with savages; the conflict of modern art with the old; the rise of the middle class; the development of capitalism and industry; the unleashing of natural forces through technology-all this belongs to the experiences or facts that are always conjured up and tied to the concept of progress and, more than that, to the progression toward something better.
>
> (Koselleck, 2002, p. 225)

This political concept expanded on other fields – *inter alia*, to the field of media change. With the advent of book printing, television and the Internet are considered as media revolutions that radically transform everything that has hitherto existed. The radical change of a revolution is the disruptive manifestation of modernity. The revolution departs from the old towards something new – which means a step in the direction of progress. This belief in progress through a radical revolution of existence is a profoundly bourgeois belief and contested by Lyotard with the term 'post-modernity.' But change does not necessarily lead to progress. For example, the urban media revolution led to a fragmented society in which the individual becomes disoriented in the face of social and media complexity. With the media change of civil society, self/ world perceptions change as well. In the course of urban modernity, avant-garde aesthetic groups formulated an anti-bourgeois critique – the cultural hegemony of bourgeois modernity and the bourgeois subject as an expression of 'the' modern are delegitimized.

4.2 From postmodernity to Bildung-based postmodern education

The concept of modernity is often extended with the concept of postmodernism. Like the term 'modernity,' the term 'postmodernity' is a rather open concept: "Postmodernism cannot be considered to be a single unified theory, nor can it be seen as a coherent set of philosophical positions" (Yaakoby, 2012, p. 10). Like the concept of modernity, the concept of postmodernity is also a 'negative' concept; that is, a concept that is based on the demarcation of something previous. "Although there are significant differences between the Postmodernist theories can all focus on the criticisms of modernism" (Yaakoby, 2012, p. 10).

On an epistemological level, Lyotard defined the term 'postmodern' in his writing "The Postmodern Condition – A Report on Knowledge" in 1979. This paper, which Lyotard wrote on behalf of the city of Québec and the university council of the government, focuses on the state of postindustrial society. According to Lyotard, modernity is characterized by unifying narratives, or social world interpretations. These narratives/world interpretations capture the social transformations teleologically as a process of progress.

From Lyotard's analytical perspective, modernity is discursively identified as the age of scientific, political, and economic systems which are ideologically based on metanarratives (cf. Niedermair, 1992, p. 87). Metanarratives such as Enlightenment or Marxism create a coherent understanding of society. The metanarratives can be understood as strategies: they place the past, present, and future in a meaningful relationship with one another. History is not experienced nihilistically but receives a teleological aspect via metanarratives. From this perspective, metanarratives are part of the self-understanding discourses of civil society: modern metanarratives reflect the 'culture of modernity.' Metanarratives are based on a value system whose components are 'universalism' and 'individualism,' as well as 'activism' and 'rationalism.' These values should unfold in a 'rational modern society.' Metanarratives constitute a monolithic offer of social coherence that guarantees claims to truth: "True knowledge [...] is always indirect knowledge; it is composed of reported statements that are incorporated into the metanarrative of a subject that gurantees their legitimacy" (Lyotard, 1983, p. 35). The postmodernity perspective is a perspective which led beyond the belief of infinite progress.

> Simplifying to the extreme, I define postmodern as incredulity toward metanarratives. This incredulity is undoubtedly a product of progress in the sciences: but that progress in turn presupposes it. To the obsolescence of the metanarrative apparatus of legitimation corresponds, most notably, the crisis of metaphysical philosophy and of the university institution which in the past relied on it. The narrative function is losing its functors, its great hero, its great dangers, its great voyages, its great goal. It is being dispersed in clouds of narrative language elements-narrative, but also denotative, prescriptive, descriptive, and so on. Conveyed within each cloud are pragmatic valencies specific to its kind. Each of us lives at the inter section of many of these. However, we do not necessarily establish stable language combinations, and the properties of the ones we do establish are not necessarily communicable.
>
> (Lyotard, 1983, p. xxiv)

Modernity stands for advance and progress. In the course of this transformation, groups are also forming that demand a new beginning that goes beyond bourgeois values, for example, Marxists.

According to Lyotard, postmodernism is characterized by a substitution of metanarratives. From this perspective, postmodernity has less of an epochal status and more so represents an attitude of mind (cf. Yeh, 2013, p. 38). The postmodern consciousness is a consciousness of an epistemological rupture. This consciousness of a rupture is defined by a relationship of tension between metanarratives and little stories. Lyotard sets the model of little stories against the metanarratives. Instead of totalizing metanarratives, a discourse 'landscape of little stories' should be created. With this landscape of little stories, a plurality of diversity emerges. Little stories function as a critical contrast to the totalizing claim of metanarratives. This subversive epistemological perspective is marked with the prefix 'post.' The 'post' in the conceptual constellation of modernity and postmodernity marks the rupture with the totalizing claims to coherence and totality of metanarratives. Through little stories, the minority receives a voice. The postmodern concept of little stories can be understood as the empowerment of marginalized groups. From this perspective, the postmodern condition is a discursive landscape of plurality. These critical, postmodern strategies of reflection are also transferred into discourses of educational theory: "The growing influence of postmodernism on academia also significantly influenced the philosophy of education" (Yaakoby, 2012, p. 10). Postmodern education bears characteristics of education: it focuses on the development of the individual in a social context. This development of the individual in a social context is realized through a tolerant self-reflexiveness.

> A tolerant self-reflexivity, a positive appreciation of the self-narration – thereby knowing about its relativity - can be seen as one of the basic educational goals of a postmodern education program. The values that constitute postmodern education are those of empowerment in the most profound meaning of the term.
>
> (Aronowitz & Giroux, 1991, p. 22)

Unlike 'modern education,' postmodern education is based on the principles of self-determination and self-directed learning. "Pluralism is a feature of postmodernism. Educationally, the art of creating and choosing is more important than ordering and following" (Hok-chun, 2002, p. 58). Accentuating the sovereignty of the individual makes postmodern education a special kind of Bildung. Postmodern education can be interpreted as a form of education-oriented pedagogy. Other interpretations are accepted and interpreted as impulses for the learning process. This openness towards the other corresponds to the educational characteristic of explorative curiosity and dialogue as a form of education-based communication. From this perspective, postmodern education continues the educational tradition of bourgeois society. When one's own thinking is a parenthetical critical of knowledge from a pedagogical perspective, this undermines an irrational claim to the totality of one's own thinking. In order to learn and educate oneself further, other narratives are needed. Without other perspectives, every educational process comes to an end.

Lyotard formulates his postmodern concept on the border between the television age and the upcoming digital age. At the time, the discourse landscape was still sharply defined by a cultural hegemony of unidirectional mass media. Little stories could hardly articulate themselves audibly as a counterpublic. In the media ecology of the digital age, a technical-social infrastructure appears in which little stories can articulate themselves. The unidirectional and polyphonic mediality of digital media enables a postmodern public sphere. This digitally based, postmodern counterpublic unfolds at least to some extent in the digital age, standing in the tradition of the counterpublic articulated in urban modernity.

4.3 The urban counterpublic of the urban avant-Garde: from Dadaism to Street Art

Avant-garde movements of modernism such like Dadaism had art reacting to the fragmented, disruptive media ecology. Dadaism especially was a reaction of the First World War and the cruelty which unfolded in the heart of bourgeois society. Avant-garde movements like Dadaism criticize the bourgeois hegemony criticized and therewith the concept of progress. Modernity is the perception of crises. The civil society itself is considered as the fractured crises. Bourgeois vocabulary is deconstructed towards a 'post-bourgeois' meaning (cf. Reckwitz, 2012, p. 289). The avant-gardes of urban modernity challenge the meaning of central notions of bourgeois self-understanding discourses. Avant-garde movements such as Aestheticism, Symbolism, Dadaism, Surrealism refer to new aesthetically oriented forms of knowledge that transcend the focus of rational cognitive knowledge, which is mediated via reading and writing. On the level of discursive meaning, the avant-gardes formulate an aesthetic questioning of bourgeois values. The questioning of bourgeois culture and values was probably most radically formulated by Dadaism.

Dadaism emerged as an avant-garde international art and literature movement around 1916.

Who used the word Dadaism first remains open. The Dadaists united artistic-political protest. The actors of this movement chose the deliberately banal-sounding term Dada for their revolt. Dadaism is the term commonly used today for this art movement (cf. Ades, 1975). The term Dada(ism) is the radical doubt about everything which is directed against the norms and culture of civil society.

> Dada is a new tendency in art. One can tell this from the fact that until now nobody knew anything about it, and tomorrow everyone in Zurich will be talking about it. Dada comes from the dictionary. it is

terribly simple. In French it means "hobby horse." In German it means "good-by," "Get off my back," "Be seeing you sometime." In Romanian: "Yes, indeed, you are right, that's it. But of course, yes, definitely, right." And so forth.

(Ball, 1916, para. 1)[4]

One can raise the thesis that Dadaism is the consequence of bourgeois epistemology. This might be a paradox, but the radical doubt, in turn, is an epistemological feature of civil society: Dadaism – like Kant's epistemology – is based on an absolute individualism and the destruction of established ideals and norms which are meaningless for the individual and their claim to freedom. According to this radical epistemology, Dadaists insisted that Dada(ism) is an open concept and thus not definable. Dadaists called for the destruction of the bourgeois order since that was what they wanted to destroy. The impressions of the First World War were inscribed in the Dadaist rejection of bourgeois culture, which was directed against "the madness of time," as the Dadaist Arp put it. It was the bourgeois who were blamed for the war. Their ideals were perceived as 'empty' and 'hollow.' As a consequence, the new, modern anti-bourgeois art rejected any rules. Absolute, relentless freedom was set against rules that prescribe how art is to be created. With the concept of the artist, the whole of bourgeois society was at stake in Dadaism. Dadaism questioned all previous art by producing intended nonsense via satirical exaggeration. Famous examples of this radical destruction are so-called sound poems that were invented by Hugo Ball. Dadaists experimented with photomontages as well as with sound poems. The result was artworks which put the concept of rationality and progress in question on an aesthetic level. Bourgeois rationality was confronted with Dadaist irrationality. The Dadaist's irrationality needed the public sphere (Ades, 1975, p. 4). Dada artists aimed to be part of the public sphere. As a – maybe understandable – radical form of counterspeech, the Dada artist protested the war as well as authoritarian bourgeoisie and artists through targeted provocations and supposed illogic. The intended meaningless works of Dadaism got their meaning through the demarcation from the 'meaning-universe' of civil society: language is emptied of its sense, and the sounds are combined to form rhythmic sound images. In deconstructing the language, the whole bourgeois order is put in question. The bourgeois order is expressed in linear sentences that structure the world in a linear-causally determined way. When the individual of book culture learns reading and writing, the individual is also encultured into the symbolic order of civil society – by destructuring or deconstructing this linear-causally determined language, the Dadaist de(con)structs the whole bourgeois value-system.

How does one achieve eternal bliss? By saying dada. How does one become famous? By saying dada. With a noble gesture and delicate propriety. Till one goes crazy. Till one loses consciousness. How can one get rid of everything that smack of journalism, worms, everything nice and right, blinkered, moralistic, Europeanized, enervated? By saying dada. Dada is the world soul, dada is the pawnshop. Dada is the world's best lily-milk soap. Dada Mr. Rubiner, dada Mr. Korrodi. Dada Mr. Anastasius Lilienstein.

(Ball, 1916, para. 3)[5]

From a learning-theoretical point of view, Dadaism is the plea to start completely new. Very traditionally, this demand was formulated on a stage – the platform of bourgeois art. Initially the center of the Dada counterpublic was Zurich. Dada artists such as Arp, Ball, Tzara, or Schwitters lived there as conscientious objectors and performed on the stage of the Cabaret Voltaire. Cabaret Voltaire was founded in February 1916, and "The Dadaist Manifesto" was read on the stage by Ball on July 28.[6]

Dadaist sound poetry[7] was performed on the stage of Cabaret Voltaire, and other avant-garde artists such as Klee, Kadinsky, and Stravinsky also had a stage there. After the end of the First World War, the Zurich group disintegrated and spread to metropolises of urban modernism, such as Berlin and Paris. In Paris the Dadaist revolt was to be brought to the attention of the Paris public (cf. Ades, 1975, p. 21). The Dada counterpublic was one of the provocative confrontations. Out of the Dada movement Surrealism emerged. As avant-garde movements, Surrealism and Dadaism rejected purely rational forms of knowledge. Beyond the chaos of Dadaism emerged the non-rational human existence of Surrealism. Dreams and delusional associations, and states of consciousness (sometimes after the consumption of drugs) formed the focus of artistic production. Like Dadaism, Surrealism rejected the logical-rational form of bourgeois culture. Brton wrote in the 1924s Manifesto of Surrealism:

We are still living under the reign of logic: this, of course, is what I have been driving at. But in this day and age logical methods are applicable only to solving problems of secondary interest. The absolute rationalism that is still in vogue allows us to consider only facts relating directly to our experience. Logical ends, on the contrary, escape us. It is pointless to add that experience itself has found itself increasingly circumscribed. It paces back and forth in a cage from which it is more and more difficult to make it emerge. It too leans for support on what is most immediately expedient, and it is protected by the sentinels of common sense. Under the pretense of civilization and progress, we have managed to banish from the mind everything that may rightly or wrongly be termed superstition, or fancy; forbidden is any kind of search for truth which is not in conformance with accepted practices. It was, apparently, by pure chance that a part of our mental world which we pretended not to be concerned with any longer – and, in my opinion by far the most important part – has been brought back to light. [8]

Surrealism, like Dadaism, was part of the bourgeois revolutionary paradigm. Breton, a central thinker of Surrealism, published the newspaper "La Révolution Surréaliste" between 1924 and 1929. Surrealism was open to new media. New media made it possible to augment reality. In the sense of surrealism, new surreal realities can and should be constructed. A cinema screening was already considered an event with surrealistic potential. One sees moving images with a real effect that is not real at the same time because it consists only of light and a flat surface.

Like Dadaism, Surrealism deconstructs writing and reading, the basic cultural tools of civil society. In the context of bourgeois self-understanding discourses, writing and reading are given the opportunity to enable a linear and thus rational structuring of the world. This linear structure is to be transcended by 'écriture automatique.' The écriture automatique is intended to open standardized forms of reflection of the reflexive self for the 'sur-real.' A central goal of écriture automatique is not so much liberation in the act of writing as much as the exploration of the sources of inspiration (cf. Bürger, 1996, p. 149). With this surrealistic method of writing one should be able to encounter a new world view that goes beyond the known reality. With new forms of writing we get to know ourselves anew. The Revolt against a social order perceived as coercion, was the will to completely transform interpersonal relationships and strive for a union of art and life (cf. Bürger, 1996, p. 12). In manifestos (i.e., in the media form of book culture) avant-garde groups like the Surrealists formulated their positions. Via these manifestos the avant-garde groups still participated in art-discourse and were part of bourgeois public sphere.

In summary, it can be said that art was – and still is – a field in which bourgeois ideas of the order are questioned by a counterpublic. Beyond the art market, the counterpublic is often formulated as so-called street art. In the 1968 movement, students painted quotes from Surrealists on the walls of Paris. And even today, as a medium of street art, walls are the canvas for an artistic, anti-bourgeois resistance. As an example for current anti-bourgeois street-art one can refer to the works of Banksy or the art of the Berlin Kidz. From 2011 to 2018, the Berlin Kidz painted statements on buildings. The Berlin Kidz formulated the messages in Pixação. Pixação was created in the 1980s in São Paulo. The 'Pixadores' wrote (tagged) their messages on the walls. Instead of graffiti, Pixação is more calligraphic, less colorful, and anti-commercial. The Berlin Kidz adapted the Pixação font and rappelled from the roofs of Berlin to attach their lettering to the buildings. In their anti-bourgeois orientation, the Berlin Kidz stand in the tradition of the Dadaist-movement (Figure 4.1). This is what 'Paradoxon' – a member of the Berlin Kidz – says in an interview with the TAZ:

Paradox: We are a group of very different people. These include sprayers, trainers, Parcours runners, but also people who only photograph and film. Which brings us all together: We want to move something. We want to open other people's eyes to social problems and the system in which we all live. That motivates us. And with this motivation, we go out and spray the walls of Berlin (own translation).

It's not surprising that the Berlin Kidz, like the Dadaists, chose the urban metropolises as a stage for their art and formulated their art there in the sense of a counterpublic. The metropolis is the stage of the public sphere. At the same time, the city is also a central discourse topos in the processes of self-representation of urban modernity. In the pedagogical discourse of urban modernity, the city advances to the appearance of the alienation experiences to which children are exposed. This happens exemplarily in the progressive education movement – probably the most influential pedagogical movement of urban modernity.

Figure 4.1 Picture of a House painted with Pixação-Letters. Below in German is written: For the people out there who miss a miracle (own photography).

4.4 Progressive education as (counter-)pedagogy of modern urbanism

4.4.1 The century of the child

The year 1900 should not just be considered the year of a media revolution that led to urban modernity. 1900 should also be seen as the year in which the *Century of the Child* began. The Italian king is said to have demanded it at his accession to the throne (cf. Elschenbroich, 2000, p. 41). In her book titled *Century of the Child* from 1902, the Danish pedagogue Ellen Kay demanded the same. This book was immediately translated into many languages.

Ellen Kay's book is a programmatic highlight of the progressive education movement. Progressive education can be defined as an international movement that began at the turn of the century and ended in Germany with National Socialism or Nazism. The progressive education movement occurred during the change from the 19th to the 20th century – especially in Western and Southern Europe (ca. 1900–1933).

From 1918, progressive educational approaches increasingly found their way into the state education system. From the mid-1920s onwards, the limits of progressive educational approaches were increasingly reflected. With National Socialism and the Second World War, the progressive educational movement came to an end. The progressive educational movement still lives on today in Waldorf pedagogy, Montessori approaches, and Freinet schools. Their approaches are also reflected in primary school pedagogy in didactic methods such as the morning-circle and free work, in which the pupils themselves should organize their work. However, as a movement progressive education is history.

The progressive educational movement lead to a new paradigm. One result of this paradigm shift in educational theory and practice is the concept of pedagogy, which focuses on the needs of the child. One consequence of the development and implementation of alternative educational practices is the search for an adequate alternate conceptual understanding of education. The different concepts which had been developed within the progressive educational movement have mostly a critical perspective on the effects of the European modernization process which led to an urban modernity.

One basic subtextual premise of progressive educational approaches can be summed up as the following: the standardization and automation of production processes is leading to an epistemic rupture in which the human being is more functionally understood and understood as 'commodity.' People are primarily perceived by society in a producing and consuming function. Against the backdrop of such a functional and alienating embedding of the individual the new concept of the child can be analyzed as a counterconcept. In the twenties, children increasingly became the motif of social protests (cf. Elschenbroich, 2000). The change of the world begins with the change of childhood. As social figures, children became the vanguard of self-liberation from economic and bourgeois-moral oppression. Childhood increasingly became a symbol of a new beginning and innocence. It is not surprising that children were photographed like little else (cf. Elschenbroich, 2000, p. 42).

One significant characteristic that unites the different forms of progressive educational concepts is a perspective on the human being that is intended to counteract 'industrialized alienation' and often is linked with an idealization of the child (cf. Oelkers, 1995, p. 34). The guiding idea was to foster holistic, individual development of the child. Subtextually the progressive educational movement stands in the tradition of a Bildung-theoretical understanding of education: to foster the child and its potential, the physical, mental, and spiritual self-education have to be supported. Thus, one characteristic feature of progressive education approaches is the goal to develop help for the child's self-education and self-determination. This idea is methodically reflected in approaches that are still practiced today, such as the 'Montessori Material.'

4.4.2 Pedagogy beyond urban metropolises

The child and their nature should be able to unfold in a world characterized by increasing industrialization and urbanization. A lot of progressive educational pedagogues criticized the alienation effects of the urbanization and moved to the land. For example, the French teacher Célestin Freinet reacts to urban modernity and its effects of alienation by a retreat to the countryside and with the requirement to integrate more nature into the urban metropolises via big parks. Hermann Lietz (1868–1919) saw Country Boarding Schools ('Landerziehungsheim') as an alternative to urbanization. While cities have a toxic influence on the development of the child, so-called 'Landerziehungsheime' should allow the possibility of holistic development. In 1898 Lietz founded a home for the lower school in Ilsenburg and one for the middle and upper school in 1901 and 1904. With the progressive education movement and its critique at of alienation of the human being within the urban metropolises, the so-called outdoor pedagogy emerged. Outdoor pedagogy can be understood as an education-oriented form of pedagogy in which, above all, action-oriented aspects are in the foreground. In principle, outdoor education sees itself as an alternative to a pure cognitive pedagogical practice. In outdoor pedagogy, learners should develop their thinking and feeling holistically. Learning content, for example, self-directed exploration, should be experienced holistically out of a so-called real situation.[9] Against the background of an emphasis on holistic experience and the learners' own activity, it is not surprising that the roots of practical concepts like the 'experiential education' lie in reform pedagogy. The first scout groups, founded in 1907 by Robert Baden-Powell, or the holistically oriented school by the sea, founded by Martin Luserke in 1925, can be regarded as precursors of experiential education.

4.4.3 Free text as a Bildung-oriented media-didactic approach

The progressive educational approaches and institutions of pedagogues such as Maria Montessori (1870–1952) and Célestin Freinet offered alternatives to state educational institutions and their teacher-centered frontal pedagogy. In the course of progressive education, action and production-oriented teaching and learning strategies were developed. Through these teaching and learning strategies, children could actively discover the world and develop themselves in the world. One example is 'free text,' developed by Freinet.

Freinet developed a pedagogical approach in which children actively and self-directedly discover the world through excursions and at the same time produce texts in which they reflect on their environmental experiences. In 1923 Freinet acquired a printing press. With the printing press, Freinet's pupils were able to publish their own written texts. This led to the creation of a school newspaper. Gradually the free texts and the school newspaper replaced traditional schoolbooks. In consequence, the press itself became the symbol of Freinet pedagogy. Freinet actively worked to improve the printing technology for his purposes. In 1926 Freinet developed a printing press for schools which he improved technically and sold in large numbers in the following years. Bildung-didactic aspects found a concrete realization here, without being identified as Bildung-didactic as such. The media-didactic concept of the free text is based on the implicit Bildung-theoretic premise that individuals learn in active and reflexive confrontation with the environment:

- Going on excursions represents the active dimension of learning, while
- reading and writing represent the reflexive dimension.

In the sense of a reflexive evaluation of one's own experiences and in consequence one's own self/world relationship, pupils can behave towards their learning *within* their environment and *in* interaction with their environment. Experience and (self-)reflection are placed in a direct context and intervened.

> Free writing must be genuinely free. This means writing only when you've got something to say, when you feel a burning need to set down in writing or in pictures something bubbling up inside you. Spontaneous writing is an activity children will do on a corner of the table late at night; on their knees, while listening to their grandmother relive the extraordinary stories of life in days gone by; on their schoolbags, while waiting to go into class; and also, naturally without prodding, during the free periods scheduled into the school day. In this way, we can be sure that the writing produced represents, in a living way, the things that most deeply stir the children's feelings, the things that mean the most to them, the things that have the most educational value.
>
> (Freinet, 1990, p. 17)

Writing about their own experiences and reading about the experiences of the other pupils provided the framework for reflection in which the pupils can thematize their own self/world relationship. In other words: learning to read and write is embedded in a reflexive experience, through which the subject can form himself in the sense of Bildung. Through the interplay with the text between production and reception, the individual can think about himself and his being in the world. The reflection should be practiced while learning to read and to write. This learning process starts with teacher-guided exercise and leads to a text entirely produced by the students themselves. At the beginning, the student paints a picture that depicts a scene of an excursion. The pupil tells the teacher the sentence the teacher should write as a subtitle. The pupil tries to reproduce the text. By practicing this, the pupil masters the written language step by step. In the sense of a production-oriented didactic, environmental experiences symbolically materialize in the goal of a text written entirely independently by the pupil. In contrast to 'school fibulae, 'which intend to recreate the pupils' world of experience in a didactically structured way, 'free text' becomes a mirror of the concrete experiences with the environment and a space to reflect about one's own self/world relationship. The process of experiencing and learning about the world is symbolically and reflexively reproduced by free text in the written language.

Fee text can also lead to a 'long-term' self-reflection in which the subject deliberately deals with his past or his 'becoming': the text I once have written will remain with me for years after completion (provided I have kept it well). Through the words the subject writes and the pictures they painted, they gain access to their former 'I' or to their former self/world relation. The construction of one's own 'narration of the life course' becomes possible through confrontation with the self-written. Development phases can be (re)constructed for the writer based on their own text production – a form of documentation which is also practiced in early childhood education in the form of portfolio work.

Summing up, one can state that Freinet's pedagogy focused on the orientation of the needs of the child. According to Freinet, learning does not serve only the purpose of acquiring competencies. Rather, the acquisition of competencies should go hand in hand with the self-unfolding of the individual. Freinet focuses above all on learning to read and write as the central cultural techniques of bourgeois society. These central cultural techniques should be learned via action and production-oriented strategies. Since Freinet sets a focus on action and production-oriented learning strategies and starts from the premise that the children should unfold himself, Freinet can be identified as a typical representative of the progressive education movement. The fact that he places such a strong emphasis on the self-determined, action and production-oriented handling of media in educational concepts makes Freinet an implicit precursor of a Bildung-didactic media literacy pedagogy. In other words, in times of urban modernity, Freinet developed a pedagogical concept that tries to give (media-)didactic answers to the challenges of urban modernity. But one has to be aware that in the course of the progressive education movement, no coherent discourse on media had been developed. The single medium (book, photograph, film) with its effects or didactic possibilities was in focus and not the question about media and education in general. In addition, a more pragmatic approach to the new technical possibilities of media was in focus; individual concepts of using media within educational contexts was more relevant than discourse about the relation between media and education. Urban modernity was a conflictual era with many tensions. In addition to criticizing alienation experiences, it contained the development of standardized entertainment culture and consumer capitalism. While reform pedagogy stood for the holistic development of the child, Fordist capitalism developed a standardized view of man. The advertising industry, which expanded and became professionalized in the consumer capitalism of Fordism, was the source of needs that were to be satisfied by consumption. From a pedagogical perspective, this process could be defined as follows: the subject appropriates needs that are not his own but become his own through an advertising-based learning process.

4.5 Fordism – the economic structure of modern urbanity

The progressive education movement provided a new understanding of the child and learning. Instead of having a deficit-oriented approach, which starts from premise that the child is defined by a lack of skills, a more Bildung-oriented approach had been developed. According to the new paradigm the child should unfold its potential via self-directed and self-determined learning processes. This pedagogical approach stands in contrast to an increasing absorption of the individual in the era of Fordism – "The concept of Fordism was popularized in the USA by Henry Ford himself and was already part of social scientific and popular consciousness in North America and Europe in the 1920s." (Jessop, 1992, p. 1).

As an economic constellation, Fordism discovered the masses as consumers. Fordism can be considered the economic constellation which emerged out of urban modernity and represents the mass culture of modern urbanity and provides its economic structure.

In the course of Fordism, the individual was constructed as a media-induced subject. The media played a twofold role here:

- On the one hand, media such as newspapers, journals, commercial films, etc. were consumed.
- On the other hand, advertising provided incentives to buy goods.

In order for the worker to become a consumer, employees had to be able to afford the products. This was achieved through technical innovations and made possible above all by the assembly line work of Fordism. In 1913, Henry Ford had the Model T car assembled for the first time. The price of the car was nearly halved from almost 600 dollars to 300 dollars (Schmitz & Daniels, 2006, p. 73). Due to this reduction, the car was affordable for the workers. Fordist 'assembly line production' rests on a radical form of division of labor.

> As a distinct type of capitalist labour process, Fordism refers to a particular configuration of the technical and social division of labour involved in making long runs of standardized goods. Fordist 'mass production' is typically based on a technical division of labour that is organized along Taylorist lines, subject in its immediate production phase to mechanical pacing by moving assembly-line techniques, and organized overall on the supply-driven principle that production must be unbroken and in long runs to secure economies of scale. The assembly-line itself mainly exploits the semi-skilled labour of the 'mass worker' but other types of worker (craft or unskilled manual workers, foremen, engineers, designers, etc.) are employed elsewhere. In addition Fordism ideally involves systematic control by the same firm of all stages of accumulation from producing raw materials through to marketing [...]. This complex technical division of labour is sometimes related to a complex regional division within or across national economic spaces.
>
> (Jessop, 1992, p. 2)

According to this process, the production of goods is divided into small work steps. Each worker carries out one work step. The assembly line sets the pace to which workers have to adapt. These processes were organized and supervised by the 'managers.' The social figure of the manager is a symbol of Fordism. A central publication in this regard comes from the mechanical engineer Taylor. In the book *Principles of Scientific Management* from 1911, Taylor analyzes how the interface between machines and people can be optimized so that the labor of the workers can be exploited to the maximum.

Due to the Fordist division of labor, production capacity increased enormously. Many goods – i.a. telephones and an electrified household – were now also affordable for the middle class, which gradually began to emerge as such. Fordist consumer capitalism was promoted by an increase in purchasing power through an increase in wages. Ford introduced the '5-dollar working day.' However, this was tied to moral standards: only 'dignified' workers were included in the five-dollar category, morally consolidated and family-bonded (cf. Resch & Steiner, 2016, p. 232). This group of consumers experienced an increase in their standard of living and also in their life expectancy. The average life expectancy of a person born in 1930 was about 61 years. Working hours in the industry were around 47 hours a week (Schmitz & Daniels, 2006, p. 65). Leisure time became a more important sphere for capitalism. With leisure time, the commodities which were produced in the working time could be bought and consumed. With leisure time the advertising industry became more important: advertising met a mass market which became purchasing-powerful through the Ford production form above all. With Fordism, the rise of advertising began (Prokop, 2001, p. 247).

4.5.1 From advertising to the culture industry

Advertising and its industry gained relevance by advertising products and providing reasons to buy a product. At the same time, advertising also made it possible to increase added value: to sell goods at as high a price as possible. Advertising has the task to create reasons that increase surplus value; in other words, advertising should motivate consumers to pay the price for the product, although the concurrence sells a similar product at a lower price. Advertising offers a strategy for this: to increase the purchase value, desires must be created through advertising. The Fordist strategy was dependent on mass consumption, and this meant that new desires for consumption had to be constantly created. So it comes as no surprise that, ever since the 1920s, Hollywood films have regularly featured the latest cars, the most modern apartments, marble bathrooms, well-equipped kitchens, chic dresses, smoking, and drinking in the most beautiful occasions (cf. Prokop, 2001, p. 330). Culture and advertising are increasingly linked with each other. Adorno and Horkheimer analyze this link with the term 'culture industry.'

The term culture industry describes a process in which a combination of autonomous art or creative culture and standard industry emerges (cf. Müller-Dohm, 2018, p. 147). Culture industry means that the aesthetic forms of societal expression in fields such as music, fine arts, literature, etc. are mass-produced as goods.

Their utility value consists in the distraction and entertainment of the recipients as cultural consumers. "Culture today is infecting everything with sameness. Film, radio, and magazines form a system. Each branch of culture is unanimous within itself and all are unanimous together" (Horkheimer & Adorno, 2002, p. 95).

At the same time, the culture industry formulates advertising messages and creates needs which can be fulfilled by buying a commodity. According to Horkheimer and Adorno this leads to a commodity-like form of self/world relation: "Films and radio no longer need to present themselves as art. The truth that they are nothing but business is used as an ideology to legitimize the trash they intentionally produce" (Horkheimer & Adorno, 2002, p. 95).

The term culture industry is also a term which formulates media criticism and influenced German discourse on media pedagogy. This media criticism is directed against the mass media of the electronic age, such as radio, and above all, against television. The main point of its criticism is a 'market-pervaded' form of reality. In other words, the way in which the mass media reproduces reality is determined by the market (Prokop, 1974, p. 87). Mass media conveys a 'commodity consciousness' to the recipients; consumption and the need for commodities are conveyed and thus a commodity-like form of self/world perception is mediated: "Rechnical rationality today is the rationality of domination. It is the compulsive character of society alienated from itself" (Horkheimer & Adorno, 2002, p. 95).

The development of social wealth through full employment, economic growth, and rising consumption levels created the external conditions for the internalization of market logic (Prokop, 1974, p. 49). This internalization of market logic manifests itself in the adoption of a lifestyle that focuses on consumption and which is mediated by the media. According to the criticism on the cultural industry, the choice between different goods is not a real choice as only different goods can be chosen. Goods and the lifestyle the goods represent are taken for granted because one is constantly confronted with them and acts blindly within the commodity form, that is, considers their rules to be completely natural and allows oneself to be influenced by their 'factual constraints' (Baumeister & Negator, 2007, p. 47). The goods themselves cannot be escaped. The result is a commodity-formed life, which is the fulfillment of desires conveyed by the media. As a consequence, individuals begin to see the world from through a commodity-shaped lens. Accordingly, the reception of products of the culture industry is shaped by preformed, standardized patterns of perception mediated via media. The individual is subjected to desires which were mediated via advertising. In *informal-accidental learning processes* we incorporate value-settings which are actually not ours (accidental learning is defined as a way of learning which emerges along with other activities and happens quasi-accidental.) One can call this 'inscription-process' an Erziehung-Process which takes places as an informal–accidental learning process.

4.6 Informal-accidental learning via unidirectional mass media

It is possible to apply Erziehung and Erziehung-constellations to the field of advertising: to 'seduce' the people to buy a particular product, the advertising sectors construct ideal images. These ideal images are represented via role models and can be analyzed as interpellations. Interpellations represent 'invocations,' or normative utterances in which normative expectations towards the individual are articulated. The utterance unfolds a socializing effect that can be worked out by analyzing subjectivation-dynamics. The subjectivation-dynamics represent the processes in which the individual adopts the interpellation and adjusts their self/world relation accordingly. The individual sets themself standards with normative demands and thus integrates the normative requirements into their self/world relationship. The integration of normative requirements into one's self/world relationship can be located between the poles of 'critical rejection' and 'affirmation.' Interpellations mostly take place on the level of informal-accidental learning.

Interpellation analysis focuses on the structure and impact of normative role assignments and the assignments of power of action to Actors.

- How are statements made into power relations? How are interpellations or normative expectations formulated? How are these interpellations ratified by interaction contexts – that is, how does the 'called' actor receive them?
- How are social attributions and requirements formulated as interpellations? How do the actors integrate these interpellations in the sense of dynamics of subjectivation into their own self/world relationship?

Advertising in Fordism is based on the power of informal-accidental learning, which is motivated by interpellations. In advertising, interpellations are formulated using role models. With the representation of the role model, comes the need to match more explicitly to the ideal image represented by the role model. To reduce the distance between oneself and the ideal image, one can buy products that are also owned by the role model.

- The role model represents the Erziehung-Goal. The advertising formulates more or less explicitly an Erziehung-Goal by displaying role models. The advertising-based interpellation is based on a value structure represented via the ideal image. Through interpellations, the value structure is virtualized. Interpellations represent and refer performatively to the set of values to which the subject should align themself.
- The person who feels the desire to buy a particular product defines themself more or less explicitly as a deficient being. To overcome the deficient status, it is necessary to buy the product. This implies that the individual is in difference to the structure of values or runs the risk of becoming in difference to this structure of values which are displayed via the role models in the advertisements. Through interpellations, the difference of the individual is marked in the value-structure. The interpellated individual is thus an individual of deficiency. The lack consists in the fact that the subject is not at one with the structure of values, or does not completely merge into the structure of values; otherwise, interpellation would not be necessary (Figure 4.2).

The act of buying the product can be considered a part of self-Erziehung. This kind of Erziehung takes place on an informal-accidental level:

- Erziehung is not explicitly acted out but is a process which is structurally a part of sending and consuming unidirectionally organized media content.

Empirically one can refer to the results of Bandura's Bobo doll experiment. This experiment was conducted in 1963, in a time television increasingly

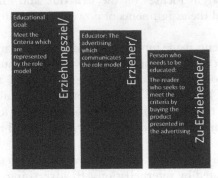

Figure 4.2 Visualization of the Erziehung-Constellation of the Fordist consumer capitalism (own illustration).

became the leading medium. In one variation of the Bobo doll experiment the age of the participants was between 35 and 69 months old and the mean age was 52 months. Of these children 48 were boys and 48 were girls. A film was shown. In this film an adult person called 'Rocky' was in a room with several objects and acted aggressively towards a large plastic doll called 'Bobo' – the doll was beaten, kicked, thrown to the ground, and insulted. In the course of this film, Rocky used new words created to insult Bobo.

The film ended in three different variations. The children were each shown a version of it. Three randomized experimental groups of participants were formed. Half of each experimental group was shown the optional end.

• In the first ending a second person joins in, praising Rocky for his behavior and rewarding him with sweets.
• The second alternative end of the film, the other person joins Rocky but blames him and punishes him with blows and threats.
• In the third ending the event remains uncommented, no other person appears.

Immediately after seeing the film, the children were individually led into a room with the same objects. The children played with the different objects and also imitated Rocky's aggressive behavior towards Bobo. They also used Rocky's neologisms. The readiness for aggression was differently pronounced in the different groups. After the incentive and reward video, the children showed a clear increase in violence. Girls especially showed more aggressive behavior towards the doll after seeing the reward. The children who saw Rocky's punishment were clearly less aggressive but showed comparable aggression after being asked to use violence. The group with the neutral ending showed similarly aggressive behavior as the group with the praise. The children were then offered a reward for each action they could remember and imitate. This increased the imitation rate in all three groups, with the group that had seen Rocky's punishment outperforming the other two groups. Bandura, Ross, and Ross establish a relation between these results and mass media:

> "Filmed aggression, not only facilitated the expression of aggression, but also effectively shaped the form of the subjects' aggressive behavior. The finding that children modeled their behavior to some extent after the film characters suggests that pictorial mass media, in particular television, may serve as an important source of social behavior"
>
> (Bandura, Ross, & Ross, 1963, p. 9)

The film sends images. These images reach the recipients, who are thereby put into a passive role. In the sense of a preliminary conclusions, it can be stated that the film mediates role models which can be interpreted as Erziehung-Goals.[10] Through interpellations, informal-accidental learning should generate needs that can be satisfied by the purchase of consumer goods. This 'learning-based' advertising strategy unfolds with a significant impact in the television era of the electronic age.

4.7 In the television era the electronic age finds its medial climax

4.7.1 The becoming of the television

The Second World War meant a break in Western political order, brought an end to the European labor movements, and, with Keynesianism and consumer capitalism,[11] brought new realities. After the Second World War, television was established almost everywhere in the world. Television represented the media change of the (Western) world and led to the climax of the electronic age. The television was both a new technology and a promising market on the one hand, and an intruder into privacy on the other. Television became the leading medium, bringing the world audio-visually into the living room. However, it took time for this to happen. While film quickly evolved from a laboratory expert to an entertainment product, the development of television has a longer history. In the first decade of the 20th century, numerous patents were filed for various television systems. In 1921, the first television pictures were transmitted across the Atlantic from a US radio station to the Parisian magazine *Matin*. In 1926, the German Reichsamt for Telegraph Technology carried out the first television tests in Germany. In 1935, the BBC began the first regular television program in London. In the same year, the first 'television room' was set up in Germany at the Reichspostmuseum in Berlin (cf. Wegener, 2017, p. 90).

Since television was not ubiquitously distributed and television sets were not yet serially produced, Germany's post set up television stations where viewers gathered (cf. Wegener, 2017, p. 90). The 1936 Olympic Games represented a first media highlight in the establishment of television and contributed to the popularity of television (cf. Wegener, 2016, p. 90).

Three years later in Germany, in 1939, an inexpensive television (the 'Deutsche Einheitsempfänger E1') was developed in order to make the new technology accessible to a broad section of the population – and to transmit Nazi propaganda into living rooms (cf. Wegener, 2016, p. 90).

On December 7, 1941, Japanese aircraft bombed the US fleet at Pearl Harbor. In consequence, the US film industry was shut down and focus was laid on war production. Television technology was used primarily for weapons technology.

After the Second World War, television began to spread. From 1952, the DDR (German Democratic Republic, or "East Germany") and BRD (Federal Republic of Germany, or "West Germany") broadcast a regular program (Wegener, 2017, p. 90). The radio stations initially took over the television technology developed by electronics companies and used the program structures of the radio for television.

Television became increasingly established, to which technical innovations also contributed. Color television made its debut in the USA as early as 1954 but was initially rejected by the population. At around 1,000 dollars, the devices were too expensive and the screens at 15–19 inches were too small. The industry reacted by launching 'Aldrich,' a cheaper television set, on the US market in 1956, which cost less than 500 dollars. From then on, television and color television spread inexorably. In 1970, there were 70 million televisions in the USA, of which 37 million were color televisions. In 1983 there were 172 million in the USA so that one can speak of a 'total television supply' (Prokop, 2001, p. 348).

Meanwhile this distribution also applies to nearly all other Western countries. In Germany, about 95% of all households own at least one television set (cf. Mikos, 2018, p. 195).

4.7.2 Fordist consumer capitalism gets a new leading media

Television, and above all color television, furthered the advertising culture of Fordist consumer capitalism. The advertising industry was strengthened above all by private broadcasters which financed themselves through broadcast advertising. The economic model of television is based on consumer capitalism and developed new infrastructures and a new advertising market. In Germany, private television began broadcasting in 1984 with stations Sat.1 and then RTL (Radioprogrammes Radio Luxemburg). These two private stations formed the basis on which the private television landscape unfolded (Prokop, 2001). At the beginning of 2015, a total of 16 private full-service television channels, 54 private special-interest channels, 80 pay-TV offers, 20 teleshopping channels and 231 nationwide regional and local television channels were counted in Germany (Wegener, 2017, p. 91).

There are pragmatic reasons for this globalization of the television market. The broadcaster reduces their risk of a lack of viewer acceptance when he buys films, series, and formats which have already been successfully broadcast in other countries (cf. Wegener, 2017, p. 92). An effect is a homogenization of the programs as can be seen in global formats such as *The Voice*.

With the establishment and expansion of television, advertising received a boost in relevance. In the 1970s and 1980s there was an advertising boom (cf. Kommer, 2017, p. 403). The increase in total advertising revenues exceeded economic growth during this period (cf. Kommer, 2017, p. 403). With the advertising boom, new advertising formats emerged: During this time, forms of advertising (e.g., sponsoring) were increasingly established beyond traditional spots and advertising. One effect is 'lifestyle advertising' which is almost entirely based on staged lifestyles. The user value of a product is less relevant than the lifestyle the product represents (Kommer, 2017, p. 403; Kergel, 2019). The figure of the social influencer, who is increasingly an advertising medium in the digital age, has its origins here.

Television pushes the economic and cultural global network of the electronic age to a climax. McLuhan speaks of a global village. Television dominated Western popular culture and general communication from the middle of the 20th century to the turn of the millennium. The television is the bridge from urban modernity and analogue mass media such as newspapers, film, and radio to the age of digital and networked media. The advertising market of the television segment is part of neoliberal deregulation and globalization. New stations led to an increased demand for programs, which was met by international exchange of programs and program formats. One effect is a new form of broadcasting and advertising which invades the living rooms. Children were discovered as a target group for consuming and advertising. One effect is a boost of media-induced informal-accidental learning.

4.7.3 Informal-accidental learning in the television era – from children's television to child persuasion

With television also began children's television started. Consider Germany as an example. A few months after the beginning of the television trial program of the Hamburger Nordwestdeutscher Rundfunk (NWDR), the children's television program started. It was April 25, 1951, and the program was led by Dr. Ilse Obrig. Obrig provided handicraft instructions, singing and melody games, reading series, gymnastics exercises, and magic tricks. Besides this explicit children's program, other programs aimed at children were broadcasted. In 1953 started the famous *Augsburger Puppenkiste* (*Augsburger Puppet Box*). 1953 also saw the broadcast of the first animated cartoons such as *Kalif Storch* (February 4, 1952) or feature films such as *Das doppelte Lottchen* (May 21, 1951; filmization of a novel by Erich Kästern; literal translation: *The Doubled Lottie*, in English: *Lottie and Lisa*). The unfolding of television can be demonstrated by the decay of the cinema. There had been a cinema boom from 1950 to 1956. In the US, Cinemas recorded a record of 817.5 million visitors. In 1961 this decreased by about 300 million (cf. Prokop, 2001).

The manipulative-suggestive impact of media in the Third Reich led to a discussion about the pedagogical dimension of the cinema. After fierce controversies, the legislative branch ratified § 6 of the 1951 law on the protection of young people in public, which was passed in 1951. One effect was that on July 27, 1957, children under the age of six were generally prohibited from going to the cinema. Television adopted these conservative tendencies. The afternoon program was restructured. Children's programs were only broadcast for 8- to 12-year-olds – although legislators had not yet given any thought to television. In the early 1960s, children's television tried to match the expectations of adults and their understanding of a decent childhood. The children were asked to engage in "meaningful" activities. In its early years the television had the role of an Erzieher.

In the following decades, children's programs developed rapidly in Germany. This development was strongly influenced by the privatization of the TV market in Germany. Children's programs such as *Sailor Moon* or *Superman* were imported from the US, and even the very young were actively involved again in the "television preschool." Cartoons and book adaptations enjoyed great popularity. In the 1990s several stations, such as Nickelodeon and the Children's Channel, were created which were fully dedicated to children. One reason was that children were discovered as an advertising group. Television programs such as cartoon series about the adventures of the MASK-Group or HE-MAN/Masters of the Universe were conceived to arouse desire and thus sell children's toys (a strategy that has not changed up to today). A look at the Masters of the Universe helps to understand the interplay of media content and the triggering of needs and wish to buy a Master of the Universe toy: Masters of the Universe is the name of an action figure series from the US toy manufacturer Mattel which was distributed from 1982 to 1988.

> As the action figure evolves so too does the expectation of 'action' inherent in the name, bringing us to the next major evolutionary step in the action figure – the Masters of the Universe line (hereinafter MOTU). While Hasbro's rival Mattel had a successful car line (Hot Wheels) and doll line (Barbie) they had no action figure lines to compete with G.I. Joe. Like G.I. Joe, MOTU action figures developed as a media tie-in, a licence Mattel had acquired for Conan the Barbarian (Universal, 1982) starring Arnold Schwarzenegger. But deciding that the movie was too violent and sexual for their target audience, Mattel took the lead barbarian character, gave him a blond Prince Valiant style haircut and placed him in a science fiction/sword-and-sorcery world. According to toy designer Roger Sweet, he was given the name 'He-Man' as it was generic enough to fit into any context.
>
> (Bainbridge, 2010, para. 28)

The "action figures" had gradually been promoted through all possible channels of the electronic age. Hasbro created a "transmedia narrative out of a web of intertexts; each figure included a booklet (later a comic) providing narrative detail on both the characters and their world (later identified as Eternia)." (Bainbridge, 2010, para. 30).

The first publications in which the background stories for the Masters of the Universe were established were mini-comics, small comic books that accompany each character. A cartoon series was broadcast from 1983 to 1984. From 1984 to 1988, the radio play series for Masters of the Universe was produced in Germany via the label *Europa*. In 1987 a real film with Dolph Lundgren in the leading role was shown in the cinema. These advertising strategies show how unidirectional media structures and advertising unfold their own media ecology to affect the recipient:

> MOTU was a massive success, rumoured to have brought in sales of $1.2 billion, earning $400 million in just three years [...] on average 11 figures were sold to every boy between the ages of five and ten in America.
>
> (Bainbridge, 2010, para. 32)

On television, the suggestive impact of radio, film, and illuminated advertising is condensed in ways never seen before. Through commercials and sent content the advertising industry exposes the individual to a unidirectional passive reception. As a result the recipients develop early a "brand consciousness." Empirically, the study of the specialized agency for child and family marketing, "KB&B – The Kids Group," provides information about the process of informal-accidental learning. The study was presented in 2017 in the run-up to the congress "Kids, Teens & Marke" ("Kids, Teens & Brands"). In March 2017, 892 children (496 girls and 396 boys) up to the age of 14 and 1755 parents (462 fathers and 1293 mothers) of children up to the age of 14 were interviewed. The results of the study show the socializing impact of brands on children's subjectivity. Children of different ages consciously perceive brands and brand images and regard them as part of their identity and identity formation. The purchase of branded goods in the categories clothing (including shoes), toys, and mobile phones is particularly essential for children. Lego and Playmobil even make it into a separate category for younger children (6–10 years), as well as Adidas for older children (11–14 years) (cf. Kbb, 2018, para. 2). Considering these results, one can speak of the socializing effect of brands, which shapes children's self/world relation via informal-accidental learning. Brands present goods in the form of "brandings" in order to increase the incentive to buy. The study shows how the commodity structure of society is socialized and therefore hardly perceived as such: "Goods are taken for granted because people are constantly confronted with them, act blindly within the commodity form, that is, consider their rules to be completely natural and allow themselves to be determined by their 'factual constraints'" (Baumeister & Negator, 2007, p. 47, translation by David Kergel).

Accordingly, the KBB study also states that brands play a prominent role in socialization: "Through brands, children and young people determine their own identity and feel they belong to a group" (KBB, 2018, para. 5, own translation).

The results of the KBB study reveal the impact of the socialization process. The brand awareness of the subject reflects the value of a commodity. This value of a commodity is created/mediated via advertising. In other words, media socialization is first of all an informal-accidental learning and effects a commodity appropriation. This leads to the fact that "for people who have been living in a society of goods producers since birth" (Baumeister & Negator, 2007, p. 47, translation by David Kergel), it is "a kind of absolutely self-evident, eternal 'necessity of nature' that 'everything has its price'." In everyday life and the resulting everyday consciousness, "the commodity is regarded as something banal that cannot even be questioned" (Baumeister & Negator, 2007, p. 47, translation by David Kergel). One can speak of an informal-accidental learning or a 'hidden' motion of learning.

4.7.4 From non-dialogical parasocial relations to images of counterpublic

The results of Bandura's Bobo doll experiment and the results of the KBB studies about the "brand-consciousness" of children both show how media can 'draw' (in German 'ziehen') children into the symbolic order of society. The empirical research on informal-accidental learning finds its counterpart in the field of theoretical research and the power-critical confrontation analysis of television. As early as 1956, Horton und Wohl analyzed the parasocial interaction made possible by television. An "as if" situation is the basic constellation of the this parasocial interaction made. This parasocial dimension is especially realized in television. The actors which appear in commercials are neither authentic, nor do they play. Often, the suggestive dimension of a parasocial relationship is fostered by a frontal speech into the camera and addressing the individual viewer. Via these strategies, television *educates* the recipients to become an audience. The recipients become familiar with their passive role. The audience becomes acquainted with societal images of what is normal and right – and what is not. At the same time, television offers a piece of security in everyday life thanks to its general and permanent availability and presence (cf. Mikos, 2018, p. 197). As long as there are commercials, there is always someone who speaks to you. This parasocial dimension of television is deconstructed by Baudrillard. In the media analysis "Requiem for the Media" Baudrillard stresses the unidirectional and hegemonic structure of electronic age´s mass media:

> The mass media are anti-mediatory and intransitive. They fabricate non-communication – this is what characterizes them, if one agrees to define

communication as an exchange, as a reciprocal space of a speech and a response, and thus of a responsibility (not a psychological or moral responsibility, but a personal, mutual correlation in exchange).

(Baudrillard, 1986, p. 280)

According to Baudrillard, dialogue – a crucial feature of Bildung – cannot unfold within the media ecology of the electronic age:

We must understand communication as something other than the simple transmission-reception of a message, whether or not the latter is considered reversible through feedback. Now, the totality of the existing architecture of the media founds itself on this latter definition: they are what always prevents response, making all processes of exchange impossible.

(Baudrillard, 1986, p. 280)

As unidirectional medium, television allows images of cultural hegemony to be transmitted. Thus, Stalder (2016) points out how homogeneous the spectrum of participants in the television discussions of the 1950s and 1960s was:

White, hetero-normally acting men, who held important institutional positions in the centers of the West, mostly spoke to each other. As a rule, they were highly specialized actors from culture, business, science, and politics. They, in particular, were legitimized to appear in public, to articulate their opinions, and to view them as relevant and discussed by others. They led the important debates of their time. Other actors and their differing positions, which of course always existed, were, with a few exceptions, either categorized as unseemly, incompetent, perverse, irrelevant, backward, exotic, or particular or not perceived at all.

(Stalder, 2016, p. 22f., translation by David Kergel)

In the spirit of media criticism of the electronic age and criticism towards Fordist consumption, a critical attitude towards mass media has also been established. Above all, protest movements in the 1960s and 1970s fought for a counterpublic to the "hegemonic power of television." The mass media of the electronic age, such as television, magazines, and radio, were perceived by the social movements of the sixties as part of the political system against which they fought (cf. Stalder, 2016, p. 70). The protesters perceived television as an institution of power, reporting as directed against them. They felt marginalized by the media and complained that their political content and demands were either ignored, defamed, or played down. One effect was the strengthening of a counterpublic sphere. This counterpublic was a new, independent public sphere that created new spaces of freedom (cf. Vogel, 2013, p. 68). However, even when the mass media of the electronic age prohibits any response and sends hegemonic images, this cultural hegemony is irritated. Images of the counterculture reach television and are able to influence social dynamics, the public sphere, and civil society's self-understanding discourses. Even as unidirectional media, television unfolded an emancipative effect and influenced among other things global protest movements. In the late 1960s and early 1970s, images from the Vietnam War and the student protests from other countries led to global solidarization effects and international politicization. The Black Panther Party is another phenomenon of counterimages in the electronic age. The representation of 'black people' has a long tradition in America. The stereotype of 'Jim Crow' inscribed into the self-world awareness of the marginalized group, as the so-called 'Black Doll experiments' revealed (see detailed below).

The social figure 'Jim Crow' represents a traditional, interpellative pattern that depicts black people in a deficit way and which can lead to subjectivation dynamics, as shown in the Black Doll experiment. In the US in the 19th century Jim Crow was the stereotype of a 'singing, lazy, slightly stupid or below average intelligent Negro,' who was mostly a slave, but still satisfied with himself and the world.

This stereotype was mainly produced in minstrel shows. Minstrels are entertainment shows. In 'Blackface Minstrels,' white people with black-painted faces (Blackfacing) created the stereotype of Jim Crow performatively. The stereotype of Jim Crow provided white workers from the industrialized north, who often did not know a black person personally, with a negative projection screen for anger and frustration. As a result of the minstrel shows, the name Jim Crow established itself as a racist term for black people. In the course of the stereotypical depiction of a Jim Crow, the actor moved his limbs clumsily so that gait and appearance resembled a crow. Hence the name Jim Crow. Another interpretation of the name refers to the song or number "Jump Jim Crow," which was performed by Thomas D. Rice. With the image of Jim Crow, a racist social figure was established.

The social figure of Jim Crow and the media representation of black people in minstrel show that performing a stereotyping, mediated representation of marginalized actors is a tradition in the entertainment industry. This tradition is continued in the so-called Buddy Movies, such as in the *Rush Hour* film series. In these formats, a stereotypical portrayal of the black man emerges, which seems to stand in the tradition of Jim Crow.

In the *Rush Hour* film series, the black American policeman James Carter is clumsy, tends to overestimate himself, and is – analogous to Eddy Murphy's portrayal of the "Beverly Hill Cops" – a 'blabbermouth.' The Chinese policeman Lee – Carter's 'Buddy' – on the other hand is portrayed as a serious, self-disciplined, and battle-tested police officer.

In pop-cultural phenomena, a symbolic order is subtextually established and interpellated, virtually invisibly. In doing so, one can fall back on an inventory of figures that was established in US-American racism. From the representation of Jim Crow in minstrel shows to "Buddy" movies, a social figure of the black man is anchored socio-semiotically. In this way, race stereotypes are created – quasi-invisibly – in a performative way. As the Black Doll experiment shows, this symbolic order inscribes itself into the discriminated subjects themselves, who experience themselves deficient against the dominant 'white' group. The subjectivation-dynamics and effect of informal-accidental learning of this media representation of black subjects can be demonstrated with the so-called 'Black Doll Experiments.'

In the 1940s, psychologists Kenneth and Mamie Clark designed and carried out a series of experiments known colloquially as the Black Doll Experiments. The aim was to investigate the psychological effects of segregation on African-American children. Four puppets were used to run the 'puppet test.' These were identical except for the color. These dolls were presented with eight questions.

> The Clarks showed young Black children a Black and a White doll and asked the children to "give me the doll that: (1) you like to play with or the doll you like best, (2) is the nice doll, (3) looks bad, (4) is a nice color, (5) looks like a White child, (6) looks like a colored child, (7) looks like a Negro child, (8) looks like you." Questions 1 through 4 were designed to disclose preferences; questions 5, 6, and 7 examined children's knowledge of differences between races; and question 8 probed children's selfidentification.
>
> (Jordan & Hernandez-Reif, 2009, S. 86)

With this questioning strategy, the demands for analytical signatures, the formulation of personal preferences, and the naming of explicitly derogatory hierarchizations merge into one another. The results show how a symbolic order with inclusion and exclusion dynamics inscribes itself affirmatively into marginalized subjects:

> Black children in the Clarks' (1947) study more often preferred to play with White dolls (67%), chose the White doll as the nice doll (59%), and chose the White doll as having a nice color (60%). Additionally, the majority of Black children chose the Black doll as being the one that "looks bad" (59%). Surprisingly, only 58% of Black children selected the Black doll as the one that "looks like you," suggesting that many did not identify with their own race. Closer examination of the data suggested that self-identification with the Black doll was related to the Black children's own skin tone, with the distribution for choosing the Black doll as looking like them being only 20% for light Black children, 73% for medium skin tone Black children, and 81% for dark skin tone Black children.
>
> (Jordan & Hernandez-Reif, 2009, S. 86)

The fact that self-awareness and self-categorization can be seen as a socializing effect is shown by the fact that self-identification as a 'black subject' increases with increasing age: "When measuring self-identification (question 8) in relation to age, only 61% of the Black 3-year-old children chose the Black doll as the one that looked like them. In contrast, 87% of the 7-year-old Black children accurately chose the Black doll as the one that looked like them, suggesting that children's self-identification with their race develops over early childhood" (Jordan & Hernandez-Reif, 2009, S. 86). Accordingly, Jordan and Hernandez-Reif (2009) in the context of the Black Doll Experiment point to the effect of interpellative subjectivations in the form of prejudices:

> The overall results from this landmark study illustrated that young Black children raised in the 1930s preferred White dolls and judged the White dolls as superior to duplicate dolls of Black skin color. Replication studies in the decades that followed revealed that White children identified with their skin tone more often than Black children [...] In contrast, Black children were inclined to reject their own ethnic group and had greater preferences for White skin tone [...] Studies also revealed that Black children were persuaded by the majority norms, values, and pessimistic judgments about their racial or ethnic group.
>
> (Jordan & Hernandez-Reif, 2009, S. 86)

The emotionally internalized values, which can lead to self-deprecation, can be analyzed as subjectivation dynamics. Interpellative patterns characterized by the devaluation of 'black people' inscribe themselves into the self-/world relationship of the subjects and can be analyzed as an effect of informal-accidental learning.

This negative stereotype was contrasted with the counterimage of "Black is Beautiful" and "Black Power." One influential organization was the Black Panther Party: In Oakland on October 15, 1966, the Black Panther Party was founded as a political self-advocacy group of black people. In the course of the founding act, the "Ten Point Program" was announced which required justice and protection for black people. The Black Panther Party's critique on racism was associated with criticism of capitalism. To protect the black community from (racially motivated) police attacks, Black Panther members with visible weapons – usually guns – followed the police. This surveillance of the government's forces of law and order was intended to prevent the police from harassing and brutally treating black citizens. This emancipative act created a counterpublic with iconic pictures. The iconic effect of armed black people, most wearing leather coats and sunglasses, was produced by the unidirectional mass media of the electronic age. The image of armed black people created a counternarrativeto the Jim Crow narrative via television. Through mass media, the iconic pictures of the Black Panther Party were disseminated on a global scale. In 1936, the Olympic Games played an important role. On October 16, 1968, the black athletes Tommie Smith and John Carlo won the gold and bronze medals at the 200-m running contest. While the US national anthem was played, both athletes raised their fists. In addition, Smith, Carlos, and Australian silver medalist Peter Norman all wore human rights badges on their jackets. The clenched fist was interpreted medially as a Black Panther party statement (Figure 4.3).[12]

Although the digital age began in 2003, unidirectional mass media of the electronic age, such as television, still have an impact that should not be underestimated. The fight for counterpublicity on TV is still an issue. As an example, one can refer to the "US National Anthem Protests" in the National Football League (NFL). At the beginning of US sports events the national anthem is played. The attendees should put their right hand over the heart – a practice that has strengthened since 2001. Since 2009, players of the NFL are required to stand by the national anthem. In 2016 the NFL player Colin Kaepernick began kneeling during the national anthem to draw attention to the issues of racial inequality and police brutality. Increasingly, NFL players joined the protests of Kaepernick. US President Trump

Figure 4.3 The raised fist was interpreted as a sign of sympathy with the Black Panther Party and, consequently, as a critique of US racism. From a media-analytic perspective, the formulation of a counterpublicity takes place in the unidirectional mass medium.[13]

called for the dismissal of kneeling US football players – with a certain effect: Kaepernick did not find a new contract. In November 2017, Kaepernick filed a complaint against the NFL and its owners, accusing them of expelling him from the NFL. In February 2019, Kaepernick withdrew the complaint after making a settlement with the NFL. These examples show how much the fight for counterpublicity in the context of unidirectional mass media is part of the discourse culture and the bourgeois public in the electronic age – and still is today.

4.8 Reacting on informal-accidental learning – media literacy, media competence and media-Bildung

With television and the associated informal-accidental learning, media pedagogical considerations became increasingly relevant. In Germany, media pedagogy gradually developed into an educational science discipline. The discussion about media literacy established itself in the US. Grafe (2011) points out that the most commonly used terms in US literature regarding basic terms in the context of learning with and about media are 'media literacy' and 'media literacy education' or 'media education.'

The word "literacy" emerged at the end of the 19th century. It has its origins in the words "literature" and "literate." The word literate was used to denote the ability to read and write. Reading and writing had become a leading cultural technology in times of increasing industrialization. The term literary bears always the connotation to be "educated." Literacy means the appropriate handling of media. It is possible to distinguish three aspects:

- technical-practical skills of handling (of e.g., formerly pen and paper as writing tools, today newer technologies and media)
- primary interpretative skills of comprehension (understanding of symbols and grammar, today also: understanding non-alphabetical and multimedia "media texts")
- secondary interpretative and critical competencies, knowledge and expertise (understanding reading, being able to include contexts for reflective evaluation and framing of the text, today, for example, reflecting on contexts about production, staging, etc. of media communication).

Media literacy is described as a result of media (literacy) education: "Media literacy is proposed as an outcome of the process media education whereby practitioners teach about media as well as through the uses of a variety of media forms and content" (Tyner, 2007, p. 524). Martens (2010) states that the competences and skills called 'media literacy' refer to aspects of analyzing and dealing with the media industry, media messages, the public, and media effects. Chen (2007) in turn attempts to present the movement of media literacy in a systematic and structured way. Chen differentiates between three phases. From the 1960s to the late 1970s, there is the "The Inoculation Phase." With the emergence of television, an attitude of preventive education initially dominates. This phase was followed by "The Facing-It Phase" from the end of the 1970s to the end of the 1980s. More power-critical positions define this phase: Popular-Cultural, aesthetic-oriented, semio-cultural, and ideology-critical aspects in the context of media literacy are thematized. According to Chen, "The Transitional Phase" followed at the end of the 1980s. This phase began at a time when the Internet was becoming an economic phenomenon. This third phase contains interaction-oriented and production-oriented guiding ideas.

In the following, the term 'media literacy' and 'critical media literacy' will be used to examine central concepts of US media pedagogy.

The concept of media literacy received crucial stimuli from a conference at the Aspen Institute in 1992. The conference focused on curricular considerations in Canada, Australia, Great Britain, and New Zealand. One of the objectives of the meeting was to attempt to pool individual initiatives for learning with and about media in the USA within the framework of a joint media literacy movement (cf. Grafe, 2011). The participants agreed on the following definition: "media literacy: it is the ability of a citizen to access, analyze, and produce information for specific outcomes" (Aufderheide & Firestone, 1993, p. 6). This definition is often perceived from the perspective of other countries as the central US definition of media literacy (cf. Grafe, 2011).

But in general it can be said, the definition of media literacy and which concrete skills and competences are needed to obtain media literacy differ according to different approaches (cf. Grafe, 2011). As a lowest common denominator, these skills subtextually aim to educate the individual into a responsible citizen. In a mediatized world, this responsible citizen should not be exposed to the media. Furthermore, the citizen should use the media sovereignly and engage discursively in the public sphere.

The discussion about media literacy can be analyzed as an effect of television as the leading medium of (post-)Fordist consumer culture. More or less explicitly, a suggestive power is attested to television. This suggestive power limits the self-determination of the subject. Against this foreign determination of media influence and television, media literacy emerges as a subfield of educational science. While media literacy is emerging in the USA as a reaction to television and its suggestive power, media pedagogy is establishing itself in Germany.

In Germany, as in the USA, media pedagogy is increasingly finding its way into pedagogical discourse with the beginning of the television age since the 1960s.[14] The starting point was the attempt to find a general term for an educational analysis of the mass media. The institutionalization of media pedagogy was preceded by a phase of media-critical reflection that was a reaction to media abuse by National Socialism. Many pedagogues after 1945 became skeptical about the media (cf. Hüther & Podehl, 2017, p. 120). One reaction to this media skepticism was media–pedagogical efforts to protect against harmful influences of the media – above all film. Since the 1960s, media education developed as a scientific discipline and established itself as a research and teaching discipline at German universities (cf. Hüther & Podehl, 2017, p. 117). Also, in the 1960s, a media pedagogical attitude was established whose target category was coined by a 'critical attitude' towards the suggestive impact of the mass media.

Since the 1980s, a more action and production-oriented approach has prevailed. Action and production-oriented media pedagogy has the goal of participatively co-designing and reshaping media (cf. Fleischer & Hajok, 2016, p. 121). The core question of media education is no longer "what does media do with the users?" but "what can users do with media?" (cf. Hüther & Podehl, 2017, p. 122).

In the course of the media transformation process, which led from the electronic age to the digital age, Baacke formulated in the 1990s the most influential media competence model in Germany's media education. The promotion of media competence has established itself as one of the central target categories of German media pedagogy.

Baacke divides media competence into four dimensions:

- Media criticism,
- Media studies,
- Media use, and
- Media design.

Media criticism is defined by three characteristics: analytical, reflexive, and ethical. Basically, media criticism is characterized by an analytical engagement with media or social processes (cf. Baacke, 2007, p. 98). Media studies, in turn, are characterized by an 'informative dimension' (Baacke, 2007, p. 99). This informative dimension contains knowledge about the functions of media systems such as journalism, broadcasting, etc. The informative dimension is supplemented by the instrumental-qualifying dimension. The instrumental-qualifying dimension focuses on the ability to familiarize oneself with new media. Together, media criticism and media studies form the dimension 'mediation.' The dimension of mediation is supplemented by the dimension of 'goal orientation.' Mediation and goal orientation result in media competence. Like the dimension mediation, the dimension goal orientation is divided into two sub-dimensions. Goal orientation is composed of the dimensions of media use and media design. Media use is made up of the sub-areas 'receptively applying' and 'interactively offering' and the dimension media design is made up of the sub-areas innovative media use ('further

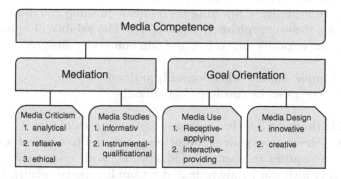

Figure 4.4 Visualization of Baacke's media competence model (own illustration).

development of the media system') and a creative dimension ('unconventional handling of media') (cf. Baacke, 2007, p. 99).

'Goal orientation' describes the action and production-oriented aspects of media use, while 'mediation' takes up the media-critical issues. Baacke's concept of media competence is linked to the pedagogical approach that all kinds of media must be considered in regard to processes of self and world-appropriation (cf. Iske, 2015, p. 251). Here one can identify a subtextual Bildung-approach (Figure 4.4).

4.8.1 Media-Bildung as a counterconcept to the Erziehung-based informal-accidental learning

Critical educational theorists like Adorno criticize the authoritarian educational/ideological process which takes place in advertising. Through culture industry, the individual adapts the worldview and value settings of a Fordist society. Durkheim pointed out that Erziehung is guided socialization. In Fordist societies, advertising ensures guided socialization or Erziehung. In Fordist civil society, advertising has the role of the Erzieher. Following this heuristic Bildung would be the counterpart of Erziehung: Bildung would mean an unfolding beyond or against the interpellations and value setting of advertising.

The authoritarian structure of advertising as Erziehung can be identified in the unidirectional structure of media through which advertising is broadcasted. A medium such as television, radio, or even an advertising poster transmits information or an advertising image to a mass group of recipients. These recipients are potential consumers whose buying interest is wanted. But the advertising does not address them as interlocutors, dialogue-partners or as citizens.

These unidirectional, Erziehung-based methods of communication can be counteracted by criticism. Criticism is an essential aspect of thinking. If we reflect rationally (i.e., if we think systematically and coherently) then we already behave critically. Criticizing means distinguishing and distinguishing with reasons (Schweppenhäuser, 1996, p. 21). The validity of opinions and beliefs can be 'critically' bracketed, and thus coherently analyzed:

• For example, are the beliefs logically justified?
• Can the premises be conclusively justified?

Reasonable thinking is to be understood as curious thinking; if curiosity is defined as a desire to experience something new and to discover something hidden, this requires an open-minded attitude. With ready-made opinions and beliefs (which can be disseminated via unidirectional media), an open-minded attitude towards the world and oneself becomes hardly possible. Conversely, an open-minded, curious perspective leads to a critical attitude towards truth claims and develops a need for dialogue. If truth claims are adopted without testing reason, this means the loss of reason, curiosity, and openness to knowledge.

Dialogical Curiosity, in turn, is a feature of Bildung. A world in which everything is shaped in the sense of a Fordist penetration of advertising, media criticism becomes an educational task. Media criticism can be understood as a categorical version of the attitude of knowledge towards the medial structure of the world. In a world in which media penetration with advertising is increasing, media criticism is becoming a task for Bildung. The penetration of the world with advertising messages captures the individual. This appropriation is shaped by the media development of urban modernity. Radio and neon signs 'teach' what the viewers' central needs are and by which products these needs are satisfied. This unification of the individual is based on the unidirectional power of the new media. The individual is exposed to the suggestive, unidirectional impact. Against this Media-Erziehung one can develop Media-Bildung as a counterconcept.

Media-Bildung enables media pedagogical theory and practice to be founded on epistemology and to be understood as a specific differentiation of educational research. The concept of Media-Bildung is defined as an epistemological reference point of media pedagogy. The normative dimension of Bildung can be understood as a reference point for the value orientation of Media-Bildung. A Bildung-oriented media pedagogy is defined by the fact that the process-related dynamics of becoming a subject in and through the use of media (in pedagogical contexts) is based on the Bildung-characteristics explorative curiosity and expectation of self-efficacy. Applying the notion Bildung to the term media in the sense of Media-Bildung, one can define Media-Bildung as the following.

Bildung takes place dialogically and requires a media structure that enables dialogical communication. With reference to this determination of the relation between Bildung and the media or media structure, Media-Bildung can be defined as a (reflexive) action and production-oriented use of media structures. According to the normative implication of Bildung, the use of media is based on explorative curiosity and expectation of self-efficacy, and (re)produces a positively connoted self/world relationship. According to this definition (Media-)Bildung is to be understood as a process. Bildung is a process which takes place in the constitution of Media-Bildung spaces via dialogical interaction.

Media-Bildung can be considered a holistic approach which escapes the concepts of Media Literacy and Media Competence and their sole focus on an appropriate *reflexive* usage of media. Media Bildung focuses on the *holistic* unfolding of the subject in the process of the media usage.

Referring to Media Literacy and Media Competence as established concepts of media pedagogy, one can say that these concepts date back to the electronic age. The focus of these concepts was an analytical examination of mass media's suggestive impact during the electronic age. These analyses remain in the context of Fordist consumer culture. The medial structure of digital media is little taken into account in the analytical perspective as the establishment of neoliberal narratives. The establishment of neoliberal narratives is inseparably linked to digital transformation. Both digital mediality and the establishment of neoliberal narratives led to new motions of learning.

Notes

1 The notion was coined by Standage, 2006.
2 Dixon Jr. was a classmate and friend of President Woodrow Wilson.
3 In Germany, radio was initially limited to the middle and higher-income groups due to high acquisition costs (*cf.* Bösch, 2019, p. 158).
4 https://www.wired.com/beyond-the-beyond/2016/07/hugo-balls-dada-manifesto-july-2016/, last accessed: 13. April 2020.
5 https://www.wired.com/beyond-the-beyond/2016/07/hugo-balls-dada-manifesto-july-2016/, last accessed: 13. April 2020.
6 A manifesto (Latin *manifestus* 'made tangible') can be defined as a public declaration of goals and intentions. These goals and intentions often possess a political orientation. As a concept in art and literary history manifestos have also been used for aesthetic programs since 1800. The formulation of a manifesto symbolically shows that avant-garde groups want to be part of the public discourse. Even radical art such as that of Dadaism is concerned with communication in deep structures, even if this communication is based on the premise of the destruction of the bourgeois order.
7 One of the most famous sound poems/poems without words is Hugo Balls "Gadji beri bimba." It plays with a percussive sounds suspends every conventionalized meaning:
    gadji beri bimba glandridi laula lonni cadori
    gadjama gramma berida bimbala glandri galassassa laulitalomini
    gadji beri bin blassa glassala laula lonni cadorsu sassala bim
    gadjama tuffm i zimzalla binban gligla wowolimai bin beri ban
    okatalominai rhinozerossola hopsamen laulitalomini hoooo
    gadjama rhinozerossola hopsamen

bluku terullala blaulala loooo
zimzim urullala zimzim urullala zimzim zanzibar zimzalla zam
elifantolim brussala bulomen brussala bulomen tromtata
velo da bang band affalo purzamai affalo purzamai lengado tor
gadjama bimbalo glandridi glassala zingtata pimpalo ögrögöööö
viola laxato viola zimbrabim viola uli paluji malooo
tuffm im zimbrabim negramai bumbalo negramai bumbalo tuffm i zim
gadjama bimbala oo beri gadjama gaga di gadjama affalo pinx
gaga di bumbalo bumbalo gadjamen
gaga di bling blong
gaga blung

8 https://www.tcf.ua.edu/Classes/Jbutler/T340/SurManifesto/ManifestoOf
Surrealism.htm, last accessed: 18 April 2020.

9 In order to redeem the pedagogical objectives of outdoor education approaches, one must make the experience usable for the everyday life of the actors through reflexive processing. For example, it can be asked how possible experiences of success can be transferred into everyday life in outdoor pressure situations.

10 The communication scientist Gerbner argues similarly. He developed the so-called 'cultivation theory.' In the 1970s, Gerbner investigated the role of television in communicating the recipients' view of the world. His thesis states that it is precisely people who watch television for several hours a day who are cultivated by television and see the world as it is conveyed on television. He thus sees television as an instance of socialization that generates distorted notions of reality among consumers.

11 Unlike liberal and neoliberal theorists, Keynes assumed that there could be 'market failure.' The economy cooling down can lead to a decline in economic growth. From Keynes' perspective, the market does not necessarily restore equilibrium by itself but requires state intervention. Keynes formulated his theory in his major work *General Theory of Employment, Interest and Money*, published in 1936, which does not assume that supply and demand on the market or markets automatically lead to an overall economic equilibrium and full employment. For example, unemployment may increase more frequently, from which the 'market forces' cannot escape alone (e.g., through wage cuts). According to Keynes, unemployment leads to lower demand for goods. Employers only hire the number of workers needed to produce the goods; the fewer goods which are consumed due to unemployment, the less demand for labor there is – which in turn causes an increase in unemployment figures. In order to break this cycle, to increase the demand for goods and to achieve full employment again in the long run, the overall economic demand for goods must increase. Here the state can intervene. The lack of private demand can be replaced by government demand, thus leading the economy out of the crisis of underemployment equilibrium. This intervention requires an increase in government spending on contracts such as road construction, rail construction, or the construction of public buildings. The new order situation creates new investment needs and thus new jobs for employers. Employees consume more again, which boosts the economy and creates new jobs. In the medium term, the state can generate more tax revenue and has to pay fewer transfer payments, such as unemployment benefits. After the Second World War public authorities followed the basic idea of Keynesianism to rebuild infrastructures that were on the ground. From this point of view, Keynesianism is based on a consumer mass culture capitalism, which was developed in the course of the establishment of Fordism.

12 Smith redefined, in his biography *Black Silent*, the meaning of his gesture. He stated that his clenched fist had been a 'Human Rights' greeting.

13 Source: https://upload.wikimedia.org/wikipedia/commons/3/3e/John_Carlos%2C_To mmie_Smith%2C_Peter_Norman_1968cr.jpg, zuletzt zugegriffen: 01. Oktober 2019.

14 Media pedagogy, as such, originated primarily in the era of television and is an effect of urban modernity. The history of the pedagogical examination of media can be schematized: The history of media pedagogy is a history of pedagogical confrontations with new media. This leads to a conservative censorship approach as well as an affirmative confrontation with new media. In pedagogues like Campe, both positions are united in one person. Campe was one of the early authors of children's literature in Germany and at the same time a critic of the reading craze.

Chapter 5

Fluid learning in the digital age

5.1 The beginning of the digital age

The digital age has replaced the electronic age. Rather than talking about 'replacement,' however, one could argue that the digital age emerged from the electronic age. Through television, images from all over the world reach us. Distances erode. Already the telegraph and later the telephone 'removed' communication. Through this implosion of time and space, the world shrinks to a 'global village' (cf. McLuhan, 1968). This implosion is decentralized by the Internet and its many-to-many communication structure. The communication potentials of the Internet were developed in the context of the electronic age and further developed in the course of the digital age and via digitization.

Digitization is the transfer of analog signals (e.g., tones, colors, measured values) into the binary code of values 1 and 0, which can be processed by computers. Digital counterparts are increasingly replacing music CDs, letters, books, keys, and paper money. The term digitization thus refers to the digital conversion of information and the digital modification of devices and vehicles. From a sociological point of view, the term digitization refers to a fundamental change that is driven by digital technology and encompasses all areas of life. One unique feature of this development is that digital media can simulate all other media. Thus, digitization also leads to media convergence.[1]

From the perspective of media history, digitization is a relatively new phenomenon. Thirty years ago, computers were hardly part of everyday life:

- In 1981 Microsoft introduced MS-DOS, and IBM presented its first personal computer (PC).
- As one of the first home computers, the Commodore 64 with 8-bit and 64 KB was launched in 1982.
- Four years later in 1986, the 'home PC' was established mainly on the electronics market as a consumer item.

In the 1980s, the Internet spread more and more internationally (cf. Döring, 2017, p. 169). The expansion of computer networks was mostly promoted in academic research. Universities and research institutions joined the Internet. With the availability of desktop computers from the mid-1980s onwards, various computer networks of hackers and hobbyists developed. The 'clubs' used the network for joint programming projects, gaming, and for social and theme-centered exchange (cf. Döring, 2017, p. 169). In the early to mid-1990s, the Internet was commercialized and thus made accessible to a broader public. The development cycles were shortened, and the mainframe computers were replaced by PCs for the office and household. The PC era was a necessary step for the rise of the Internet. However, at a time when computers were achieving their place in life, the development of the Internet was still a project known only to experts. In contrast to today, the development took place outside the public sphere – although at that time, the decision was made to make changes for the Internet:

- In 1980, the ARPA-Net was converted to the TCP/IP protocol and
- In 1983, the US Department of Defense declared TCP/IP to be the standard for its computer networks – in addition to the standardization of the written language to a national language and the establishment of the Morse code as the standard language for telegraphy, further standardization was achieved here in the course of the establishment of technical innovations.

The history of the Internet is also a history of new forms of interaction and communication that continue the networking of the electronic age. From 1979, the civilian, non-military use of the Internet was mainly reserved for researchers at US universities such as Stanford University (Stanford Research Institute), the University of Utah, and the University of California. In 1983, approximately 4000 computers were part of the ARPA Net, which was replaced four years later by the National Science Foundation Net (NSFNet). It was around this time that the term 'Internet' emerged to signify the 'network of networks.'

From 1988 through the beginning of the 1990s, the Internet was further developed: public and private networks were interconnected. The Internet had finally reached a global dimension and experienced a surge in innovation:

- In 1990, the National Science Foundation decided to open the Internet for commercial use. In the same year, the first commercial Internet provider ('World') entered the market.
- In 1993, the National Center for Supercomputing Applications (NCSA) launched the first graphical browser.

- 1993 was also the year in which the European Centre for Nuclear Research (CERN) set up the so-called World Wide Web for the public.
- 1996 – the year in which Netflix was founded – the English term Internet was included in the German Duden (cf. Döring, 2017, p. 164).

In the times of early commercialization, Internet development progressed and the World Wide Web was introduced. As innovation, the WWW stood in a discursive tradition which thematized the Internet as an alternative communication platform, beyond the capitalist logic of exploitation. Originally, the WWW was planned as an exchange platform for researchers:

> The World Wide Web (W3) was developed to be a pool of human knowledge, which would allow collaborators in remote sites to share their ideas and all aspects of a common project. Physicists and engineers at CERN, the European Particle Physics Laboratory in Geneva, Switzerland, collaborate with many other institutes to build the software and hardware for high-energy research. The idea of the Web was prompted by positive experience of a small 'home-brew' personal hypertext system used for keeping track of personal information on a distributed project. The Web was designed so that if it was used independently for two projects, and later relationships were found between the projects, then no major or centralized changes would have to be made, but the information could smoothly reshape to represent the new state of knowledge. This property of scaling has allowed the Web to expand rapidly from its origins at CERN across the Internet irrespective of boundaries of nations or disciplines
>
> (Berner-Lee et al., 1994, S. 792).

Tim Berner-Lee developed the Hypertext Markup Language (html), a programming language that enabled uniform formatting of documents. In parallel, he developed the Hypertext Transfer Protocol (http), which regulates the transfer of documents. "HTTP is a protocol for transferring information with the efficiency necessary for making hypertext jumps. [...] HTTP is therefore a simple request/response protocol" (Berner-Lee et al., 1994, S. 794). Meanwhile the spread of the Internet continued:

- In 1994, one year after the introduction of the WWW, the first commercial browser (Netscape Navigator) was launched.
- Also in 1994, the number of commercial Internet users exceeded the number of scientific users.

The development of commercial potential has accompanied the development of technological infrastructure:

- Amazon was founded in 1995,
- Netflix was founded in 1996, and
- in 1998, Google launched its service as a search engine.

5.2 Early counterculture of the 1990s net utopists

From the early years up to the commercialization of the Internet, the Internet was the space for countercultures. Cyberspace emerged with the Internet. Cyberspace, in turn, was thematized as a post-national, anarchistic space of freedom. According to the so-called 'cyberutopists' or 'net utopists,' cyberspace is an electronic space beyond any state regulation. With cyberspace, the Internet was discursively thematized as an alternative societal space:

> Virtuality need not be a prison. It can be the raft, the ladder, the transitional space, the moratorium, that is discarded after reaching greater freedom. We don't have to reject life on the screen, but we don't have to treat it as an alternative life either. We can use it as space for growth. Having literally written our online personae into existence, we are in a position to be more aware of what we project into everyday life. Like the anthropologist returning home from a foreign culture, the voyager in virtuality can return to a real world better equipped to understand its artifices.
>
> (Turkle, 2011, p. 263)

The net utopism of the 1990s stood in a grown tradition of resistance narratives in the short history of the Internet. In 1986, the hacker 'The Mentor' (alias Loyd Blankenship) published 'Hacker Manifesto – The Conscience of a Hacker.' The Mentor describes the state of digital freedom as an ecstatic experience:

> And then it happened... a door opened to a world... rushing through the phone line like heroin through an addict's veins, an electronic pulse is sent out, a refuge from the day-to-day incompetencies is sought... a board is found. 'This is it... this is where I belong...' I know everyone here... even if I've never met them, never talked to them, may never hear from them again... I know you all...
>
> (The Mentor, 2004, para. 9)

The cyberspace of the Internet opens a space for new forms of communication. These new forms of communication are 'powerless' and anarchistic.

Ten years after the publication of the "Hacker Manifesto," Barlow published the "Declaration of Independence of the Internet" in 1996 – the year Netflix was founded, and the word Internet found its way into the German dictionary. The "Declaration of Independence of the Internet" begins with the words: "Cyberspace, the new home of Mind. On behalf of the future, I ask you of the past to leave us alone. You are not welcome among us. You have no sovereignty where we gather" (Barlow, 1996, para. 1). According to this "Declaration of Independence," cyberspace is not structured according to law but is characterized by a free anarchist communicative practice (ibid., para. 4 & para. 6). This anarchist practice of free communication is beyond "race, economic power, military force, or station of birth" (ibid., para. 7).

The work *Life on the Screen: Identity in the Age of the Internet* (1995/2011), published by the social psychologist Turkle, can be understood as a – post-structuralistically influenced – approach to placing the Internet in the symbolic order. The Internet is seen above all as an opportunity to escape from subjecting effects and inscriptions, from power-structural integration. This is what Turkle writes in her book about online-based multiuser computer games (MUDs):

> The anonymity of MUDs – one is known on the MUD only by the name of one's character or characters – gives people the chance to express multiple and often unexplored aspects of the self, to play with their identity and to try out new ones. MUDs make possible the creation of an identity so fluid and multiple that it strains the limits of the notion. Identity, after all, refers to the sameness between two qualities, in this case between a person and his or her persona. But in MUDs, one can be many.
>
> (Turkle, 2011, S. 12)

According to Turkle's considerations, the constraints of bourgeois society on the individual in which every individual has his place and an individual in every place constitutes the individual as a monad of social hierarchies, can be escaped on the Internet:

> Today I use the personal computer and modem on my desk to access MUDs anonymously, I travel their rooms and public spaces [...] I create several characters, some not of my biological gender, who are able to have social and sexual encounters with other characters. On different MUDs, I have different routines, different friends, different names.
>
> (Turkle, 2011, S. 16)

This idealization of the free space that enables 'multiple' and 'fluid' identity constructions is reminiscent of Deleuze's reflections on the transcendence of the constraints of individualization, which Turkle also points out:

> Thus, more than twenty years after meeting the ideas of [...] Deleuze, and Guattari, I am meeting them again in my new life on the screen [...] In my computer-mediated worlds, the self is multiple, fluid and constituted in interaction with machine connections.
>
> (Turkle, 2011, S. 15)

Medially, the Internet enables new forms of social interaction. Turkle uses Deleuze's established metaphor of the fluid to describe strategies for escaping the fixation of the individual in social space, the fixation of the individual in hierarchical and dependent relationships:

> Individuation is no longer enclosed in a word. Singularity is no longer enclosed in an individual [...] You see, the forces of repression always need a Self that can be assigned, they need determinate individuals on which to exercise their power. When we become the least bit fluid, when we slip away from the assignable Self, when there is no longer any person on whom God can exercise his power or by whom He can be replaced, the police lose it. This is not theory.
>
> (Deleuze, 2004, S. 138)

Following on from Deleuze and regarding Turkle, the Internet can be understood as a space that enables new 'modes of life.' And new "[m]odes of life inspire ways of thinking; modes of thinking create ways of living" (Deleuze, 2004, p. 66). Against this background, organizations form which can be read as a topic of freedom and resistance, as seen in hacker groups like Anonymous and their orientation against Internet censorship and solidarity with Wikileaks. The use of the first-person plural in the motto included at the end of Anonymous messages is symbolic of the release of Anonymous' compulsions of individualization:

> We are Anonymous.
> We are Legion.
> We do not forgive.
> We do not forget.
> Expect us.

The socially fixed ego, to which Foucault referred in his conception of power, dissolves into the anonymous plural that the Internet makes possible.

Cyberspace makes it possible to conceptualize the Internet as a space of freedom, in which identity patterns become 'fluid,' individual resistance is transcended to a resistance of the digital swarm, and subalterns are given a voice. Assange updates this narrative when he contrasts a dialectical tension between cyberspace and the material-physical world:

> Once upon a time in a place that was neither here nor there, we, the constructors and citizens of the young internet discussed the future of our new world. We saw that the relationships between all people would be mediated by our new world, and that the nature of states, which are defined by how people exchange information, economic value, and force, would also change. We saw that the merger between existing state structures and the internet created an opening to change the nature of states.
>
> (Assange in Assange et al., 2012, p. 2)

In the tradition of anarchist theory, states are interpreted as structures of domination. "First, recall that states are systems through which coercive force flows" (Assange in Assange et al., 2012, p. 2). Assange concedes that states can have a democratic appearance when factions that are part of the state power apparatus are in conflict with each other: "Factions within a state may compete for support, leading to democratic surface phenomena" (Assange in Assange et al., 2012, p. 2). However, these democratic processes remain on the 'surface,' while the deep structures of state power fix basic hierarchies and dependencies: "Land ownership, property, rents, dividends, taxation, court fines, censorship, copyrights and trademarks are all enforced by the threatened application of state violence" (Assange in Assange et al., 2012, p. 2f.). From this perspective, the image of the free space of cyberspace has a discursive relevance for negotiating the possibilities of the Internet. Beyond the historical accuracy of this original history, cyberspace points to a potential space of freedom.

This discourse, which interprets the Internet as a space for counterculture, resistance, and free communication, continues to exist today in the so-called 'Deep Web' or 'Dark Web,' and in hacktivist groups such as Anonymous or Wikileaks. With the increasing commercialization of the Internet, however, a more commodified form of online-based communication has prevailed – as can be seen from the phenomenon of Web 2.0.

5.3 Web 2.0 – or the beginning of the digital age

A discursive change in the way the Internet is addressed and used is the so-called Web 2.0. Web 2.0 is a redefinition of (commercial) possibilities of the Internet after the so-called 'dotcom bubble.'

The media coined the term 'dotcom bubble' for a speculative bubble that burst in March 2000. The so-called dotcom companies of the New Economy were particularly affected by this crash and it led to asset losses among small investors, especially in industrialized countries. The dotcom crash was a worldwide phenomenon and a consequence of the first 'hype' about the commercial possibilities of the Internet. Shortly after this hype had ended, a new hype arose around the Internet and its commercial possibilities. The keyword of this hype is 'Web 2.0.' The term Web 2.0 describes the possibility that the user can quickly produce content – even without programming knowledge. Users can 'register' themselves on the Internet. Web 2.0 is based on 'User Generated Content Technology' (cf. Lehr, 2012), which enables users to interact with the Internet and create content without programming knowledge. Using Web 2.0 tools such as wikis, podcasts, and blogs as well as social networking sites (SNS) such as Facebook or Instagram, users create content in communication with other users. In other words, the term Web 2.0 refers to the poly-directional, user-centric dimensions of the Internet. Web 2.0 is not a technological revolution, it is a "social revolution" (Downes, 2005, para. 26).

Social media is a symbol of this change from 'Web 1.0' to 'Web 2.0.' People are becoming increasingly involved in identity management on SNS such as Facebook, Twitter, Snapchat, and Instagram. Via SNS, users can connect and exchange information. Social media such as SNS "became informal but all-embracing identity management tools, defining access to user-created content via social relationships" (Mitrou et al., 2014, p. 2). Web 2.0 and the associated communication culture laid the foundation for the Internet as we know it today:

- Apple launched the first legal music download service in 2003.
- The platform Flickr.com was founded in 2004 and enabled the publication of images with short comments.
- In the same year, Facebook was founded and one year later (2005), YouTube launched.
- Google Earth was also launched in 2005 and would later be followed by Google Maps and Google Street View.
- 2006 was the year that Twitter entered the SNS market.
- In 2007, Amazon introduced the Kindle e-book reader and
- Apple presented the first iPhone. The iPhone marked the beginning of the era of smartphones and mobile digital devices – three years later, the first iPad was introduced.
- 2009 saw the launch of WhatsApp – now the most popular app in the world.
- One year later in 2010, Instagram was founded and
- Snapchat was introduced in 2011.

The Social Web, as we know it today, took shape with Web 2.0. Thus we can speak of the birth of the Digital Age with the emergence of the Web 2.0 and the Social Space. With the Web 2.0-based Social Web the Internet was more than an add-on but became in the course of some years the central platform for social interaction (the development was fostered by an improvement in the technological infrastructure and the establishment of high-speed Internet.) In the Social Web, the user is transformed from a consumer into a producer or fulfills both functions as a "prosumer" (cf. Gaiser, 2008).

> The paradigm of Internet had changed: from static, isolated repositories of information shifted to dynamic, user-driven and participatory sites. Users are now able to interact with other people, create, redistribute or exchange information and opinions, and also express themselves in virtual communities.
>
> (Mitrou et al., 2014, S. 1)

In summary, it can be said that after the dotcom crash, the Internet emerged as we know it today. Between 2000 and 2013, most of the services and devices that shape our digital lives were introduced to the market. This phase of the emergence of the global, commercially-based Social Web can be defined as the beginning of the Digital Age.

With Web 2.0, the entire discourse on communication changed. Since Web 2.0, the use of digital media has restructured our world. Via Web 2.0 communication platforms, SNS such as Facebook, Google+ and Instagram, Twitter, Snapchat, and LinkedIn, users are integrated into the Social Web. Via this integration into the Social Web, the individuals become a social co-ordinate in the Digital Age. The embedding into the Social Web changes the social environment and thus our communication practices: As users we are confronted with an ephemeral stream of status messages and timelines. The deeper structures of this new media ecology are defined by the neoliberal restructuring of economics, social policy and our socio-cultural lifeworld.

5.4 From neoliberalism to neoliberal digitization

The establishment of neoliberalism deeply influenced the development of the Internet since its commercialization. Digitization is unfolding in an age of neoliberal politics and neoliberal thinking. The beginning of this phase can be traced back to the year 1980:

- Thus Prensky (2001) defines every person born since 1980 as a digital native. Digital natives have grown up with the process of digitization and are accustomed to the mediatization process of digitization.
- At the same time, 1980 is the year in which Ronald Reagan's neoliberal policies began to change the Western welfare state in the long term.

Neoliberalism replaced Fordist consumer capitalism. And neoliberalism also changed the forms of informal-accidental learning. This thesis will be discussed later and requires a clarification of what exactly is meant with the term neoliberalism. With this precise definition it is possible to analyze the connection between neoliberalism, digitalization, and informal-accidental learning in the Digital Age.

5.4.1 The unfolding of 'real-existing' neoliberalism

Besides the more Marxist-oriented critique of the mass culture of Fordist consumer capitalism, Keynesianism was criticized above all by representatives of neoliberal positions. This criticism was formulated at a time of crisis Fordist economic activity and Keynesian economic policy. A crisis of the 'consumer-oriented' capitalism of Fordism and Keynesianism led to the establishment of neoliberal economic activity and thought that continues to this day. The starting point was the slowdown in the economic growth of Western industrial nations in the 1970s. This slowdown in economic growth could not be offset despite government stimulus programs. One reason was the effects of globalization. In the 1950s and 1960s, the productivity of the Japanese and German industry grew and increasingly competed with the

American industry. With the increased global productive power, overcapacities and oversupplies were produced. As a result, prices for products fell, and US firms entered a 'profitability crisis' (Srnicek, 2017); inflation increased, as did unemployment. As a consequence, Fordism was followed by a phase of economic crisis, also known as 'Post-Fordism.' In the course of the establishment of new computer technologies, production processes were restructured. The rigid, inflexible assembly line production – characteristic of the Fordist phase – was abandoned in favor of more flexible modes of production (cf. Prokop, 2004, p. 52). The function of the qualified, skilled worker or expert in the production process was upgraded. At the same time, jobs of the middle class and the upper-lower class were rationalized away (cf. Prokop, 2004, p. 52). These changes finally marked the beginning of the neoliberal economic activity.

Neoliberal thinking in turn established itself even during Keynesian economic policy. Conceptually, neoliberal approaches see themselves in the tradition of the bourgeois understanding of freedom. The bourgeois individual should not be determined by others, neither politically nor economically. Against the backdrop of fascism, national socialism, and the state-communism, neoliberalism sees itself as an economic-theoretical representation of the freedom of the individual. The academic and theoretical thematization of neoliberal positions prepared the ground for the 'real-existing neoliberalism.'

Real-existing neoliberalism was installed in Chile, following Pinochet's military junta's 1973 coup against President Salvador Allende. Under Pinochet's leadership, a catalog of economic and political measures was implemented, which was essentially developed by graduates of the University of Chicago (Biebricher, 2012). Milton Friedman – one of the figureheads of neoliberalism alongside Hayek and a professor at the University of Chicago – traveled with students and the 'Chicago Boys'[2] to Chile to examine the implementation of neoliberal politics. Neoliberal economic policy in Chile was based, among other things, on opening up the market to foreign investors and reducing government spending by reducing welfare state benefits or 'rolling back' the welfare state. State ownership and social programs were privatized, price controls were lifted, and markets were deregulated. These measures are central features of neoliberal economic policy.

However, the USA, not Chile, should be named as the influential main arena of neoliberal politics. The starting point was the election of Ronald Reagan as President of the USA. Social services, such as Medicaid and Medicare, were cut back. State stock exchange and banking supervision, antitrust control, and trade union rights were reduced or canceled. As in Chile, there have been far-reaching privatizations. As a result of Reagan's presidency, taxes on profits and wages were lowered. Hospitals and prisons were privatized as well as parts of the military sector. The neoliberal rollback of the US welfare state was continued by other US presidents regardless of party affiliation.

In Europe, Great Britain became a pioneer in the neoliberal transformation of the Western welfare state. From 1979–1990, Margaret Thatcher was

Britain's Prime Minister and with her 'Thatcherism' brought about a neo-liberal change analogous to 'Reaganomics.' Thatcher – parallel to Reagan's economic policy – led the dismantling or privatization of central government companies such as railways, water and wastewater, aviation, coal, and steel. It is estimated that the proceeds of these privatizations of formerly state-owned enterprises from 1979 to 1996 amounted to 70 billion pounds sterling. In 1998 the value of these companies was estimated at 206 billion pounds sterling (Kergel, 2020). With the establishment of this rollback, the trade unions' right to strike was also restricted by several laws, thus weakening the voice of the workers. Another effect of neoliberal policy was deterioration of state infrastructures due to privatization. The reason for this was that an investment in the infrastructure would have run counter to maximizing profits. For example, the privatized railways saw an increase in accidents and delays, while prices increased. One consequence of the neglected infrastructure was the need for state subsidies and an expensive buy-back of the state-owned companies that had been sold. The introduction of neoliberal politics was adopted by 'Third World' countries as well as by other European states.

5.4.2 From free market to precarity

When one speaks about neoliberalism one is "generally referring to the new political, economic and social arrangements within society that emphasize market relations, re-tasking the role of the state, and individual responsibility" (Springer et al., 2016, p. 2). Springer et al. (2016) stress that "Neoliberalism is a slippery concept, meaning different things to different people" (Springer et al., 2016, p. 1). Nevertheless, it is possible to provide a basal definition of this term: Neoliberalism can be defined as an ideology which focuses on the beneficence of the free market. Accordingly, Springer et al. (2016) point out that "[m]ost scholars tend to agree that neoliberalism is broadly defined as the extension of competitive markets into all areas of life, including the economy, politics, and society" (Springer et al., 2016, p. 2). According to neoliberal thinking, free market is the best platform for people to unfold their potential and therefore should be deregulated to the greatest possible extent:

> For neoliberals, there is one form of rationality more powerful than any other: economic rationality. Efficiency and an 'ethic' of cost-benefit analyses are the dominant norms. All people are to act in ways that maximize their own personal benefits. Indeed, behind this position is an empirical claim that this how all rational actors act. Yet, rather than being a neutral description of the world of social motivation, this is actually a construction of the world around the valuative characteristics of an efficiently acquisitive class type.
>
> (Apple, 2006, p. 60f.)

The neoliberal worldview and policy focus on the liberty of the individual. This liberty of the individual was the main neoliberal argument in the end of the 1970s and 1980s. Neoliberal approaches promise the freedom of the individual in contrast to communist systems and fascism. The focus on the individual and their freedom makes neoliberal thinking compatible with the leftist emancipative concept of the subject. In the course of the increasing proliferation of neoliberal policy and neoliberal narratives, the leftist ideals of the 1960s and 1970s were discursively transformed. The neoliberal subject receives the aura of an emancipative subject-formation: "It is not difficult to find an echo here of the denunciations of hierarchy and aspirations to autonomy that were insistently expressed at the end of the 1960s and in the 1970s" (Boltanski & Chiapello, 1999, p. 97). The ideals of autonomy and freedom provided the discursive frame in which the "new neoliberal spirit of capitalism" (Boltanski & Chiapello, 1999) could unfold itself.

> Thus, for example, the qualities that are guarantees of success in this new spirit – autonomy, spontaneity, rhizomorphus capacity, multitasking (in contrast to the narrow specialization of the old division of labor), conviviality, openness to others and novelty, availability, creativity, visionary intuition, sensivity to differences, listening to lived experienced and receptiveness to a whole range of experiences, being attracted to informality and the search for interpersonal contacts – these are taken directly from the repertoire of May 1968.
>
> (Boltanski & Chiapello, 1999, p. 97)

In the course of this new, neoliberal spirit of capitalism, the role of the government is mainly considered to support the free market, and that leads to a critical view on the concept of the welfare state (Biebricher, 2012). That leads to an increase of precarity – or stable instability for the employees: "The contemporary neoliberal era is marked by an exponential expansion of contingent, flexible and precarious labor markets" (Mahmud, 2015, p. 1). This kind of employment situation fits to the neoliberal premise of deregulation of the economy: "In the neoliberal era, debt sustains aggregate demand amidst precarious labor markets and facilitates assemblage of risk-taking entrepreneurial subjects responsible for their own economic security. The result is pervasive existential precarity" (Mahmud, 2015, p. 3).

5.4.3 Becoming an entrepreneurial self

In order to establish themselves on the neoliberal labor market, individuals must become entrepreneurs. As entrepreneurs, they sell themselves as goods on the neoliberal (labor) market. In other words: the individual becomes the entrepreneur of himself. In order to survive in this market, the individual is forced to optimize himself continually.

Bröckling summarizes this human image of neoliberalism with the concept of the entrepreneurial self. The entrepreneurial self performatively reproduces the neoliberal concept of freedom. The "ideal model for the future is the individual as self-provider and the entrepreneur of their own labour. The insight must be awakened; self-initiative and self-responsibility, that is, the entrepreneurial in society, must be developed more strongly" (Bröckling, 2015, p. xi).

The entrepreneurial self is characterized by freedom and autonomy. But instead of unfolding itself within an economic solidarity and according to emancipative leftist ideals, the neoliberal subject unfolds itself as an entrepreneurial self within neoliberal freedom and is thus defined by permanent activity and "sporting competition" (Bröckling, 2015, p. 77). Like Deleuze said, it is not about finishing but about starting always anew. The main interpellation is that "[e]veryone should become an entrepreneur [...] Success at this can only be measured against the competition and therefore only temporarily" (Bröckling, 2015, p. 77). Consequently, the neoliberal subject as the entrepreneurial self is embedded in processes of permanent active competition. With reference to the neoliberal concepts of the subject it's possible to identify the underlying neoliberal structures of the Social Web. The Social Web is the digital sphere of neoliberal narratives.

5.4.4 The new digital spirit of capitalism

Neoliberal digitalization is characterized by the 'new spirit of capitalism.' This new spirit of capitalism integrated the demands of the 1968 protest movement. The student protests of 1968 demanded anti-capitalist ways of life: instead of living a life marked by Fordist consumer culture and alienated work, they demanded the idea of a self-determined life and not-alienated work. Instead of standing at the assembly line, they demanded a culture of work in which people develop according to their 'needs.' These demands are absorbed by capitalism, leading to a 'new spirit of capitalism'.

With reference to the management-literature of the 1990s, Boltanksi and Chiapello provide a discourse-analytical study on the change of the self-understanding discourses of capitalism. One main result of their study was the observation that capitalism developed a new spirit. This new spirit of capitalism absorbed the critique which was formulated in the course of the emancipation movements within the 1960s and 1970s:

> Thus, for example, the qualities that are guarantees of success in this new spirit – autonomy, spontaneity, rhizomorphus capacity, multitasking (in contrast to the narrow specialization of the old division of labor), conviviality, openness to others and novelty, availability, creativity, visionary intuition, sensitivity to differences, listening to lived experienced and receptiveness to a whole range of experiences, being attracted to

informality and the search for interpersonal contacts – these are taken directly from the repertoire of May 1968.

(Boltanski & Chiapello, 1999, p. 97)

In order for the leftist and originally anti-capitalist demands to take the form of a new spirit of capitalism, the critique of alienated labor had to be detached from the demands for social justice. The leftist, emancipative notion of freedom which combines alternative culture and anti-capitalistic critique was absorbed by a capitalistic self-understanding discourse. As a result, the alternative anti-authoritarian counterculture lifestyle and the anti-capitalist critique were detached from each other. In the course of this transformation a new spirit of capitalism emerged. This new spirit was based on the concept of an artistic-anarchistic individual: "It is not difficult to find an echo here of the denunciations of hierarchy and aspirations to autonomy that were insistently expressed at the end of the 1960s and in the 1970s" (Boltansky & Chiapello 2007, p. 97). This new spirit of capitalism is still vivid in the so-called Start-Up Aesthetics (cf. Kergel, 2020) and the concept of the entrepreneurial self.

One might ask how the social-cultural transformation of neoliberalism is linked to the digital age. One interesting link is the temporal overlap with the development of digitalization.

The Internet promises on a semiotic level a flexible, unconventional space for economic adventures. It is the ideal space where the flexibility and autonomy of capitalism's new spirit can unfold. A symbol of this flexibility in the digital age are start-ups.

Start-ups represent

capacity, multitasking (in contrast to the narrow specialization of the old division of labor), conviviality, openness to others and novelty, availability, creativity, visionary intuition, sensitivity to differences, listening to lived experience and receptiveness to a whole range of experiences, being attracted to informality and the search for interpersonal contacts.

(Boltanski & Chiapello, 2007, p. 98)

With these features Boltanski and Chiapello describe the new spirit of neoliberalism. But these features can also be read as characteristics of start-ups. Thus, the new spirit of capitalism is discursively reproduced in the concept of start-ups. Start-ups like Airbnb and Uber have a discursively rebellious attitude towards established business models and seem to stand in the tradition of the emancipatory movements of the 1960s and 1970s. One main business model of start-ups is to challenge and overcome established, authoritarian business models. These business models are mostly attacked with the platform model which has been developed within the alternative culture of the 1960s, 1970s and 1980s. As an example one can refer to Airbnb. Instead of booking an anonymous hotel room, the users have the option of an experience, 'being attracted to informality' and making 'interpersonal contacts' while renting an apartment. By renting an apartment instead of a hotel room, the user saves money. Airbnb in turn has an economic profit because they provide the platform. Finally, the owner of the rented apartment receives a little extra money. In this constellation everyone acts as an entrepreneurial self at the expense of established structures (in this case the hotel). With reference to this example one can conclude that the neoliberal new spirit of capitalism and the entrepreneurial self are inscribed into the digital economy.

The leftist demands for autonomy, self-determination, individual freedom, and non-alienated work unintentionally fostered neoliberal ideology. The fact that in the 1980s "neoliberal ideas" prevailed was also because "some of the values, procedures, and methods propagated by the new social movements have been detached from their political context" (Stalder, 2016, p. 33). In Silicon Valley, the new spirit of capitalism was condensed in the digital age. For example, the pop-cultural resistance culture of the student movements in Silicon Valley was mixed with the capitalist logic of exploitation. "Even in the 1960s and 1970s, the Bay Area radicals were still the pioneers of the political attitudes and cultural style of the new left movements around the world" (Barbrook & Cameron, 1995, para. 6). A counterculture was developed here, which was later absorbed by the new spirit of capitalism. On one hand, there was rebellion against the cultural limits of Fordist consumer culture. Thus "campaigns against militarism, racism, sexual discrimination, gay fear, mindless consumption, and environmental pollution" (Barbrook & Cameron, 1997, para. 6) were organized. These topoi were integrated into a neoliberal narrative. In the California Bay Area of the late 1960s and early 1970s, an 'amalgam' was formed. This amalgam consisted of individual performance enhancement techniques with roots in the military research laboratories of World War II, aspirations for drug-induced expansion of consciousness, and countercultural ideals of individuality (cf. Kaerlein, 2018, 103f.). This amalgam or rather this "peculiar fusion of countercultural practices and computer-technical implementations is indirectly due to the image change of the computer" (Kaerlein, 2018, p. 104). This new culture and aesthetic are precisely expressed in Apple's design language. Barbrook and Cameron point out the neoliberal implications of this amalgam and summarize it analytically in the term 'Californian ideology.' Californian ideology is defined by a neoliberal worldview in the context of the emerging digitalization and represents a new spirit of capitalism:

> Although the ideologues of California celebrate the libertarian individualism of the hippies, they never discuss the political or social demands of the counter-culture. Individual freedom is no longer to be achieved by rebelling against the system, but through submission to the natural laws of technological progress and the free market.
>
> (Barbrook & Cameron, 1995, para. 17)

The digitization leads to a perfect neoliberal market. Thus, in the

> version of the Californian Ideology, each member of the 'virtual class'
> is promised the opportunity to become a successful hi-tech entrepre-
> neur. Information technologies, so the argument goes, empower the in-
> dividual, enhance personal freedom, and radically reduce the power of
> the nation-state. Existing social, political and legal power structures will
> wither away to be replaced by unfettered interactions between autono-
> mous individuals and their software.

The neoliberal model of an 'electronic marketplace' characterizes Californian
ideology, which is based "on a strong concept of the individual that with the
help of information technology he can live out his – especially economically
estimated – freedom (cf. Kaerlein, 2018, p. 112). The model of the entrepreneurial self takes on a digital form here: For the often-freelance programmers,
designers, and advertising experts of Silicon Valley, the boundaries between
work and leisure become blurred (Kaerlein, 2018, p. 112).

5.4.5 The neoliberal dimension of the social web

Fordist capitalism is transferred into the performance logic of neoliberalism.
The neoliberal market is a market for consuming neoliberal evaluation. The
interactions that arise through consumption are subject to constant evaluation.

It is a consumer of freedom inasmuch as it can only function insofar as a
number of freedoms actually exist: freedom of the market, freedom to buy
and sell, the free exercise of property rights, freedom of discussion, possible
freedom of expression, and so on. The new governmental reason needs freedom therefore, the new art of government consumes freedom. It consumes
freedom, which means that it must produce it. It must produce it, it must
organize it. The new art of government therefore appears as the management
of freedom (Foucault, 2008, p. 63).

In the Social Web, the individual stages himself in the sense of 'personal
publishing.' He narrates himself on the Social Web as successful, or as a successful entrepreneur of himself. The user of SNS like Instagram consumes the
content or data of others and in turn produces data himself. The user is thus
both consumer and producer of content and in this interaction, becomes a
'prosumer.' The Social Web or SNS are for many the Internet as such; some
users move only on Social Web. Therefore, one can speak of an SNS universe
(from Latin *universus*, as 'the whole'). But this universe knows limitations
and borders: Social Web media such as Facebook, Twitter, LinkedIn, or Instagram are based on closed standards. These closed standards are controlled
by network operators (cf. Stalder, 2016, p. 214) and form the boundaries
of the expanding Social Web universe. Standards users are prevented from

communicating beyond the boundaries defined by providers; in other words, Facebook can only be used to make contact with other users of the platform (cf. Stalder, 2016, p. 214f.). Digital capitalism is based on the networking of service providers and service users. A network is more attractive when more individuals connect (cf. Stalder, 2016, p. 231). This logic leads to a competition in which the bigger network is thus more powerful. At the end of this development, the network effect becomes a monopoly effect (cf. Stalder, 2016). In the battle for the network effect and the monopoly, users are locked into the respective network.

The networks form small universes. In these networks, users narrate themselves as entrepreneurial selves. These self-narratives on SNS are written for evaluations. The Facebook thumbs up represents a performance benchmark for a successful self-narration. Its social impact can measure the quality of self-narrations. The Facebook thumbs up, like similar variations on other SNS, represents a "digitized gesture signaling approval, approbation, agreement, praise, or even on occasion a reminder to the receiver of the sender's existence" (Faucher, 2013, p. 1).

Valuations are a crucial element of SNS. Some social-psychological studies thematize social pressure, which can unfold in the Social Web universe. For example, Bak and Kessler (2012) show that Facebook-users react according to normative aspects. Individuals who use intensive Facebook, 'like' a picture more, when it has been 'liked' already and thus got a positive appreciation by other users. And Nadkarni and Hofmann (2012) point out that individuals engage themselves in Facebook because of a need for belonging and the need for self-presentation. The communicative structure of SNS effects an intersubjective surveillance regime: "Every social media user can be equally observer and observed, controller and controlled" (Mitrou et al., 2014, p. 12). Andrejevic (2005) terms this phenomenon "peer-to-peer monitoring" (Andrejevic, 2005, p. 48). According to Andrejevic peer-to-peer monitoring can be defined as "the use of surveillance tools by individuals, rather than by agents of institutions public or private, to keep track of one another, covers (but is not limited to) three main categories: romantic interests, family, and friends or acquaintances" (Andrejevic, 2005, p. 488).

This peer-to-peer monitoring on SNS is complemented by the rating system on commercial digital platforms. On commercial digital platforms such as Airbnb or Uber, customers and providers valuate each other.

In the consumer culture of Fordism, the spheres of leisure and work were still separate. During working hours, consumer goods were produced that were consumed during leisure time. The unidirectional mass media of the electronic age were supposed to seduce people into consuming. In the age of neoliberal digitalization, users are more actively integrated as consumers. They produce data in the networks, which is then resold to companies for personalized advertising. Instead of receiving idealized role types, as was still the case in the electronic age, users stage themselves as entrepreneurial selves. The spheres of leisure and work are increasingly intertwined. As entrepreneurial selves, the ideal image of the neoliberal role model is met. This leads to new business models, such as social influencers. In the case of social influencers, the sphere between self-narration and entrepreneurship finally erodes. Beside social influencers as prototypes of entrepreneurial selves in the sphere of the Social Web, there exists another example of the interplay between leisure and work on the Social Web. In 2012 on behalf of Careerbuilder, an online job portal, Harris Interactively interviewed 2,303 HR managers on the importance of social media in recruitment procedures. The recruiters stated that they would also check the applicant's social media activities to check the applicant's suitability. The primary source was Facebook, with 65%, followed by LinkedIn with 63%. One of the criteria was whether the applicants fit in with the company's image:

- When asked why they use social networks to conduct background research, hiring managers stated the following:
- To see if the candidate presents himself/herself professionally – 65 percent
- To see if the candidate is a good fit for the company culture – 51 percent
- To learn more about the candidate's qualifications – 45 percent
- To see if the candidate is well-rounded – 35 percent
- To look for reasons not to hire the candidate – 12 percent (Careerbuilder, 2012, para. 7, H.i.O).

34% of recruiters who had already used SNS to check a candidate's data indicated that they found information on the profiles that led them not to hire the candidate. The reasons range from uploading inappropriate content to the fact that candidates lied about their qualifications:

- Candidate posted provocative/inappropriate photos/info – 49 percent
- There was info about candidate drinking or using drugs – 45 percent
- Candidate had poor communication skills – 35 percent
- Candidate bad mouthed previous employer – 33 percent
- Candidate made discriminatory comments related to race, gender, religion, etc. – 28 percent
- Candidate lied about qualifications – 22 percent (Careerbuilder, 2012, para. 10, e.i.Oo).

29% of recruiters stated that they found information on an applicant's profile that had a positive impact on their recruitment. The reasons are given for the positive impression range from intuitive assessments to positive feedback posted by other users about the applicant:

- *Good feel for candidate's personality – 58 percent*
- *Conveyed a professional image – 55 percent*

- *Background information supported professional qualifications – 54 percent*
- *Well-rounded, showed a wide range of interests – 51 percent*
- *Great communication skills – 49 percent*
- *Candidate was creative – 44 percent*
- *Other people posted great references about the candidate – 34 percent* (Career-builder, 2012, para. 12, e.i.o.)

This study shows how the spheres of work and private life are becoming intertwined increasingly. The assessment of one's private life becomes a job recruitment factor. Willey et al. (2012) assume that the "utilization of social network sites for applicant screening will continue" (Willey et al., 2012, p. 307; see also Chiang & Suen, 2015). Applicants are aware of such assessments. This can be illustrated by the results of a study by Martensen, Börgmann, and Bick (2011). The study examined "the impact of SNS on the employer-employee relationship." One result of the study is that the "members of SNS do believe that (potential) employers carry out research on the Internet and that users behave accordingly" (Martensen, Börgmann & Bick, 2011, p. 252). Among other things, SNS users were asked whether they would use the Internet as a platform for self-narration aimed at potential employers: "[T]he 228 respondents (60.7%) agreed with the following statement: The Internet enables me to present myself the way I want to (n=376, μ=3.59, σ=0.78)" (Martensen, Börgmann & Bick, 2011, p. 250). In summary, it can be said that we must not speak of digitization but a neoliberal digitization of the world of life and work. In the Social Web Universe, users create profiles, produce data, and evaluate each other. This Social Web universe can be understood as an expanding field of neoliberal enterprises.

5.5 From stratification as Bourgeoise equality to algorithmic determination

5.5.1 From stratification as Bourgeoise equality

A central element of bourgeois emancipation is the political demand for equality. Equality is discursively formulated as an ethics-based political demand. In the modern understanding of morality and politics, the idea of securing freedom and equal rights for all takes precedence over securing the privileges of social elites. In demand for equality, the political participation claims of the bourgeoisie manifest themselves on a political-ethical discourse level. In addition to a critical, ethical perspective on orders of status, the demand for equality refers to the process of standardization that has been ongoing since modern times. This process of standardization is part of the rational measurement of the world, in the course of which bourgeois society institutionalizes itself as a rational society. This measurement is based on standardization reasoning that compares phenomena to each other via categories.

Phenomena are ordered and categorized through terms. The dissective embodiment of the world through the instrumental reason of the natural sciences has effects on world views. This is due to the fact that new thinking during the Renaissance and the Enlightenment emerged first in the natural sciences, turning away from old dogmas and towards empirical experimental methods. The act of empiric categorization led to the numerical measurement of the human being in modern times, which has been expanding since the 19th century and covers almost every area of life. In this way, people are stratified as elements that can be standardized – because they are comparable – as social coordinates, and in doing so, birth and mortality rates are measured based on categories such as health, life expectancy, birth, and death rates.

With categorizations and an increasingly taxonomic understanding of the world, standardization thinking lays the foundation for the modern development of statistical procedures. The processes of secularization also influenced the development of statistical methods. An example of this can be seen in the development of probability theory. Originally, the elaboration of theories about probability was confronted with the idea that the uncertainty of a future event was a divine attribute that people would never be able to control – unless they consulted God (cf. Desrosières, 2005, p. 52f.). The establishment of probability theory presupposed a secular-rational approach to chance. As a procedure by which the rationality of decisions in uncertain situations can be justified (cf. Desrosières, 2005, p. 51), probability theory replaced a sacral handling of chance. Already in antiquity, dice and lots were not only used in games of chance; they were also meant for divination, for investigation of the divine will, and at best for determining the future. The invocation of a deity was expressed in the drawing of lots to decide particularly delicate disputes (cf. Desrosières, 2005, p. 53). This was founded on the conviction that the random outcome indicated the will of God to the doubting person (cf. Desrosières, 2005, p. 51).

The development of probability theory shows exemplarily how (bourgeois) processes of secularization make new forms of knowledge generation possible. These standardization forms of world-appropriation were established in a context of power imbalances and relied on them as control and power technologies. This standardization stratification was established in the second half of the 18th century as a power technology. It was not directed at the body but at the collective body of a population. Individuals became social categories; the population was turned into a 'biological whole.' This laid the foundations for the technologies of power which Deleuze analytically formulated using the concept of control society: control can be achieved through standardization. Individuals can be broken down into divisible and relational elements that have their place in abstractions or categories of taxonomic orders.

Through stratifying processes, individuals and their actions are recorded as data. Through the act of standardization, data form the basis for numerical control. This numerical control consists of ciphers or numerical signs that represent information through masses, samples, data, and markets. With the secular standardization of civil society, discipline and training are replaced by regulation and control. The (civil) state functions as the controlling authority. The collection of demographic data on the population and the tabulation of wealth, as well as statistical surveys on life expectancy and of illness, are the strategies of order and control.

5.5.2 Stratification as Bourgeoise equality in the digital age – data tracking and echo chambers

Digital data continue the tradition of measuring the individual in bourgeois society and carry control as a technology of domination into the digital age. In general, a standardizing measurement of individuals through 'bio-power' generates supra-individual knowledge of power. This standardizing measurement is often coupled to a commodity-based measurement of the individual in the context of bourgeois society. In the digital age, this standardizing, commodity-based survey is characterized by an integral dialectic of digital governmentality and economic exploitation of the digitally recorded individual.

In the course of neoliberal digitalization the modern measurement of the individual unfolds a hitherto unknown power of action – which in turn points to the continuities of bourgeois society. With the establishment of the digital age, companies such as Google or Facebook are increasingly becoming the medium to quantify standardization of individuals. In addition, digitization is refining surveying techniques, as can be seen from the phenomenon of 'big data'.

Big data results from online data, customer data, and user-generated content as 'unstructured data' (contents of e-mails and SMS messages, etc.). It also arises at the interfaces of automated data processing. The big Internet and communications companies are the main drivers of an enormous accumulation of private data and its evaluation for economic purposes. Big data is a commodity of the globalized media economy and digital society is no longer free to decide whether it wants to escape this availability (cf. Kammerl, 2017, p. 44).

In the course of data traffic in the Social Web, users leave digital traces. Every click I make is stored. Every step I take is traced. The data become the digital shadow of our movements in the Internet. The recording of the digital data shadow is done routinely and goes unnoticed. Data tracking is part of our regular social operations. The paradox of an 'ephemeral fixation' of the individual emerges. As one example of such an 'ephemeral fixation' of the individual, one can refer to tracking cookies. In principle, cookies can be described as a small text file that enables the webserver to recognize visitors to a website. In general, cookies are used unnoticed by the user on sites that switch on advertising or have interactive functions. In principle, a distinction can be made between session cookies and tracking cookies.

The first cookies are used for online banking: if the session expires, the cookie and the session ID stored by the cookie also expire. Ad servers use so-called tracking cookies. When one visits a website on which advertising is placed, a tracking cookie is stored in the browser by the advertising banner via the ad server. Tracking cookies enable the user's behavior to be tracked and analyzed.

Each time an online visitor returns to Facebook, the server that generated the cookie can check and read what was previously written to the file, for example, which pages were accessed during the last user session.

By identifying the interests and preferences of the users, personalized advertising can be implemented. By selecting content, information is sorted and filtered. This leads to bubble phenomena and echo chambers: users are shown information that corresponds to previous Internet use. They are isolated in a "bubble." The openness of knowledge is structurally limited by algorithmically determined content. The digital space of the Internet is transformed from the freedom space of cyberspace into an echo chamber that is structured by algorithmic procedures and reproduces worldview via personalized content and advertisement: "Because most of Google's revenue is derived from advertising, it is important to consider advertising as a media practice with tremendous power in shaping culture and society" (Noble, 2018, p. 105).

5.5.3 The algorithmic determination

Through the Social Web, the individual is fixed or located. One effect of this localization is the pre-configuration and restriction of digital freedom of movement. Algorithmic configurations delimit movement. Through 'algorithmic procedures,' a whole range of social classifications are enforced. Originating in the field of mathematics and programming, algorithms can be described as logically structured 'solution plans' or calculation rules. An algorithm consists of defined instructions or predetermined steps that must be completed in order to accomplish a task. They formulate specifications to ensure that specific results and output data are realized for certain inputs. Consequently, an algorithm is defined by the fact that it is determinate: the same inputs lead to the same outputs when they are repeatedly executed. At the same time, the algorithm is deterministic because each step is predefined. In search engines like Google, search terms or keywords act as input data. The search engine algorithm delivers the results and arranges them according to ranking criteria. However, search engine algorithms such as Google's PageRank are constantly being changed:

> It is based on mathematical theorems consisting of numbers and formulas. Within the Social Web, algorithms provide a technically determined frame of reference and preference. The seemingly objectivity of algorithms should no obscure the reproduction of re-production of power

structures via algorithms: In 2015, U.S. News and World Report reported that a 'glitch' in Google's algorithm led to a number of problems through auto tagging and facial recognition software that was apparently intended to help people search through images more successfully. The first problem for Google was that its photo application had automatically tagged African Americans as 'apes' and 'animals'. The second major issue reported by the Post was that Google Maps Searches on the word 'N*gger' led to a map of the White House during Obama's presidency, a story that went viral on the Internet after the social media personality Deray McKesson tweeted it.
(Noble, 2018, p. 6)

Through the algorithmic structure of personalized content, unidirectional hegemonic images are produced. These hegemonic images create an authority that inscribes itself in the individual through informal-accidental learning. The media structure of the digital falls behind its participatory possibilities and reproduces a receiver-transmitter structure of the electronic age. One can speak of objectivistic learning in terms of digital algorithm-structured pictures.

5.5.4 Digital algorithm-structured pictures and objectivistic learning

The objectivist paradigm assumes the existence of objective knowledge with which the world can be explained: From this perspective, meaning is something that exists aside from experience. This perspective leads to the learning goal of mapping this objectively given reality as accurately as possible to the internal representations of the learners. Since this reality is given independently from the persons living in the world and therefore independently from consciousness, one can make statements about the existing objects that are objectively true or false. Cognitivism, like behaviorism, assumes a single, objectively true reality.

The entire execution of the lessons and the presentation of content has a distinctly organizational and systematic character, so that learners take over the objective knowledge from the teacher in a ratio of 1:1.

Teaching and learning follow the assumption of so-called 'knowledge transport.' In frontal teaching, knowledge is transmitted. Using the learning theoretical perspective as a heuristic approach, one can interpret the mediation of hegemonic pictures as an objectivist form of learning.

In other words, an objectivist epistemology is pursued through the production of hegemonic images. Hegemonic images appear as a normative ideal state. The receiving individuals are confronted with them. This approach, which was early used in the Fordist advertising industry, is increasingly evident in the digital production of ideal images and stereotypes. The phenomenon of social influencers[3] is paradigmatic for this form of influencing action through hegemonic images and idealized stereotypes. From a sociology-semiotic perspective, the buying behavior impacted by social influencing allows us to conclude how hegemonic images have a subjectifying effect. If users or followers let themselves be influenced in their buying behavior by influencers, an affirmative attitude towards the hegemonic images can be concluded.

A study by the Bundesverbands Digitale Wirtschaft (BVDW, German Digital Industry Association) shows that influencer marketing is successful.[4]

According to the study, almost one in five Germans has already bought a product because it was recommended to them by an influencer. For men, the proportion is lower at 17%, for women slightly higher at 22%. Among young consumers between 16 and 24 years, the percentage is much higher at 43%. The study further differentiated the group of respondents. For example, the market researchers wanted to know how often the respondents come into contact with influencers on social media. The study showed that the conversion success, that is, the purchase decision based on recommendation, increases with the frequency of communication. Of the 41% of respondents who stated that they had contact with influencers at least once a week, almost every other respondent aged up to 45 years had, according to the study, already purchased at least one product. The influence of influencers falls drastically in the age groups over 45 years. In terms of behaviorist learning theory, we can interpret the consumer behavior of the followers as a learning effect. The stimulus is the advertising of the influencers.

5.5.5 The structural equivalence of commodification

(Control) state access to the citizen and the capitalist exploitation of the individual are intertwined. It could be said that a transformation of state bio-power into the psycho-power of the market is taking place. In order to substantiate this thesis of a merging standardization and commodified appropriation of the bourgeois subject as a technology of domination, the following section will use Adorno's concept of commodification as a supporting argument. Adorno refers to a structural equivalence between a taxonomic, standardizing way of thinking that relates things to each other and makes them comparable, and the thinking figure of the commodity.

When things become commodities, this means that things assert their ability to be standardized through money, which acts as an intermediate medium of exchange. It is through money that things relate to each other as commodities. Money classifies the value of goods so that things of different kinds can be brought into a comparative relationship with each other. From a socio-semiotic perspective, the ethical demand for equality also enables quantitative standardization: at the moment when all individuals are equal, they are also comparable with each other. This can be seen most clearly in the everyday act of grading. The grades artificially generate a 'performance gap' that corresponds to market logic. The graduate with better grades has more opportunities to establish himself in the labor market. In other words, social bonding forces have been transferred to the market.

The establishment of comparability is a characteristic of secular-critical reason and a basic principle of capitalist circulation of goods. From this perspective the history of capitalism and the history of the epistemology of the West are closely intertwined. This structural equivalence requires a radicalization of standardizing thinking, which has subjectivizing effects and shapes patterns of thought. Thus, the industrial standardization reinforces the tendency to stereotype thinking. Collective, discursively pre-figured identity patterns are constituted by a commodity-shaped standardization of opinions, world views, and political positions. These identity patterns are conveyed by consumer goods which, in the sense of the Marxian concept of fetish, have an identity-creating semiotic attached to them. Adorno speaks here of the phenomenon of commodification, meaning the commodified socialization of the subject. Consequently, according to Adorno, commodification refers to the extension of logics of exploitation to areas that are not originally contextualized by capitalist profit increases and profit maximization. The objects acquire a commodity character, for example, by making them comparable with one another through numbers.

Something becomes a commodity when it can be exchanged for other goods in a market. The exchangeability presupposes a uniform measure that makes the goods comparable with each other. Through the abstraction of comparison or through the operation of abstraction, the singular or the incomparable is lost. In an identification that is based on an equality and interchangeability of one person with the other, the individual becomes a commodity. Through this act of 'egalitarianism,' the human being as a commodity-shaped, subjectified individual is denied singular or unique forms of self-determination and self-articulation. This commodification is cross-field and manifests itself also in the so-called 'culture industry' of Fordism.

5.5.6 Multiple choice identities and commodity

Through integration into the Social Web or SNS, the individual is produced as a social coordinate in the digital age. Communication platforms such as Instagram and Facebook, as well as Google+, Snapchat, and LinkedIn, reproduce conventionalized identity patterns. SNS organize people into multiple-choice identities.

Starting with the process of registration, which marks the entry into a SNS, the human being is measured in a standardizing way as an individual through subjectivations.

This raises questions about who owns identity and identity makers in cyberspace and whether racialized and gendered identities are ownable property rights that can be contested. One can argue [...] that social identity is both a process of individual actors participating in the creation of identity and also as a matter of social categorization that happens at a social-structural level and as a matter of personal definition and external definition.

(Noble, 2018, p. 104)

Thus, as a rule, when registering for an SNS, primary identity data such as age, profession, and gender must be provided, which constitute the (bourgeois) individual in the space of transcendental epistemology or within taxonomic tableaus.

> The registration process has remained very simple, but once registered, users are continuously faced with prompts to provide personal information, which enables them to be categorised [...] Power is made manifest on Facebook in various ways: the constant prompts, urging users into self-revelation; the constant threat of exclusion, if users do not provide access to personal information; and the lack of control users have over their own information and content.
>
> (Buchanan, 2011, S. 275f.)

Digital Evaluation constitutes a control regime in which the users and their feedback have a disciplinary effect on other users. In this way, monitoring by the companies is flanked by monitoring by the customers.

This is exemplified by the neoliberal logic of evaluation in the digital age. In Fordism, the customer was still king and could evaluate services. In the neoliberal spirit of the digital age, customers and service providers assess each other.

When satisfaction is assessed with five points or ten stars, the smartphone becomes an algorithmic supervisor. Feedback as 'quality measurement' becomes the decisive control instrument.

In the rating system used by Uber, both the driver and the passenger give a mutual assessment of their behavior (cleanliness of the vehicle, driving behavior, friendliness, and punctuality) by awarding between one and five stars (maximum) for the other side of the market. If the driver's average rating falls below a certain level, he will not be considered as a driver in the future (cf. Peitz & Schwalbe, 2016, p. 11).

The employees receive digital feedback, which can also be understood as a performance assessment in the sense of behaviorism. Based on the feedback, the users have the possibility to reorient their actions to optimize their behavior and thus themselves or their entrepreneurial self.

5.5.7 Selection by consequences – digital feedback as behavioral learning

With reference to Skinner, one can speak of a 'selection by consequences.' The basic paradigm of behaviorism is the stimulus–response scheme. In essence, certain stimuli (so-called stimuli, e.g., hunger, light) are followed by specific reactions (so-called responses, e.g., salivation, turning towards the light source).

In behavioristic models, learning is understood as amplification and weakening of behavior. If a specific behavior results in a pleasant event (e.g., praise, reward, or learning success), this behavior is reinforced. This process is called positive reinforcement. On the other hand, if a specific behavior transforms an unpleasant state into a pleasant state, and this also strengthens the corresponding behavior. In other words, according to behavioristic learning theory, learning emerges by providing information and reinforcing the desired behavior. Stimulus-response chains form the basis of learning according to behavioristic principles. This means that specific reactions follow certain stimuli. As soon as a stimulus-response chain has been established, the learning process is over, and the learner has learned something new.

Digital feedback can be described as learning by consequences. Likes and comments are instant feedback on behavior.

5.6 From Mobile Internet to the era of post-digitality

The Internet era of Web 2.0 brought the Social Web. For many, the Social Web is synonymous with the Internet in general. With Web 2.0 and the Social Web, a neoliberal digitalization unfolded. This phase, which follows the Web 2.0 phase, can be described as post-digitality.

The next media/digital transformation of the Internet took place with the establishment of the 'mobile Internet.'

The term 'mobile Internet' or 'mobile web' refers to the establishment of an Internet connection via mobile digital devices such as smartphones, tablets, or laptops.

The development of mobile (digital) devices such as smartphones can also be traced back to the 1980s. In 1983, Motorola produced the basic model of a mobile phone, which cost around 4000 dollars when it was launched on the market. Ten years later, the mobile phone became marketable. Motorola was again a pioneer, followed by Nokia and Siemens, who also introduced mobile phones. It was at this time that the first 'Proto-Smartphone' came onto the market: IBM's Simon Personal Communicator (SPC) of 1992 comes closest to what a smartphone is today. The SPC had a touch screen, was email-enabled and could fax, but did not have a web browser. Due to the short battery life (approximately one hour) and high price, the SPC was not able to establish itself on the market – but the development of smartphones had begun. The mainstream market was now focused on the introduction of mobile phones:

• At the end of the 1990s, mobile phones were equipped with SMS functions, address lists, and organizers.
• At the beginning of the 2000s, more and more mobile phones with cameras were produced for the mass market.
• The introduction of the iPhone in 2007 meant the birth of smartphones.
• The following year, Samsung and HTC built smartphones with the Android operating system.

An improvement in technological infrastructure accompanied the development of mobile digital devices:

- The first commercial Internet connection with mobile phones was offered in Finland in 1996.
- In Japan, unlimited Internet surfing with mobile phones was only possible with the i-mode mobile phone service since 1999 (see Chatfield, 2013, p. 74f.).
- Mobile Internet was also introduced in Germany in 1999 when technology with 9.6kb/sec was presented at CeBIT in the form of WAP (Wireless Application Protocol).

Since then, transmission speed has massively increased. LTE (Long Term Evolution) achieves a data transmission speed of 300mbit/sec. One effect of these technical innovations was the spread of the mobile Internet, as can be seen by the development of mobile Internet -usage in Germany. The number of smartphone users in Germany rose significantly from over six million in 2009 to 49 million in 2016. During this time, mobile data traffic in Germany multiplied from 11.47 million gigabytes to 65.41 million gigabytes. In 2015, data traffic reached 591 million gigabytes. 2014 was the first year in which more young people went online with a mobile digital terminal than with a desktop PC (see Feierabend, Plankenhorn & Rathgeb 2014). These developments had a lasting impact on our media environment; the ubiquitous Social Web has developed as we know it with mobile Internet. A characteristic feature of this is that the distinction between the virtual world of cyberspace and the material–physical world implodes. With the establishment of mobile Internet, the virtual world of the Internet inscribes itself into the material–physical world. The process can be analyzed with the term 'augmented reality.' The use of digital devices is not only a technical but also a social phenomenon.

5.6.1 The quantified self of the post-digital era

Social software applications such as Facebook are often used for self-portrayal and thus fulfill a social function. The digitally–enhanced augmented reality is also a socially–changed reality, and is structured by neoliberal narratives that have established themselves in the Web 2.0 age. In this context, the mobile Internet is an extension of the medial reality of the Social Web as it has established itself in the Web 2.0 age.

With mobile Internet and mobile digital devices, the media structure of reality is changing. The Internet has become an 'Internet to go,' enabling new social practices such as the 'selfie culture.' The result is a 'post-digital age,' defined by the (in)visible omnipresence of the digital in the physical-material world. The smartphone is the symbol for this media change. The mobile phone is a symbol of the Internet's ubiquitous presence in the physical-material world. With the smartphone, the digital is so omnipresent that it 'disappears' in everyday life through its omnipresence. With the media ecology of post-digitality new social practices are emerging. One example of the post-digital penetration of digital media is the culture of self-tracking, or digitally-based self-measurement and lifelogging.

The term 'self-tracking' refers to the practice of measuring one's own activity with the help of activation trackers such as fitness wristbands. This way steps, calorie consumption, and sleep can be recorded among other metrics. In other words, mobile sport trackers and fitness trackers are miniaturized computer applications that are mainly used for physical training. In general, self-tracking or lifelogging is about tracking and recording human life in real-time by digitally measuring body, behavior, and data traces and storing the data for later retrieval.

As with the development of the Internet, DARPA[5] plays a central role in the development of digital logging. For example, the LifeLog project was designed to develop equipment for soldiers. The soldiers were to receive, among other things, a mini-camera attached to the helmet, two microphones, and a GPS tracking system.

As a technical innovation, self-tracking is a social practice that has a semiotic and cultural dimension. In the course of establishing neoliberal narratives, the concept of self-measurement via mobile digital devices reflects the self-optimization of the entrepreneurial self. The individual uses his freedom for self-optimization through self-tracking. At the same time, one's physical activities can be captured and optimized through self-tracking. The relationship to the body is not primarily defined by feelings and emotional self-evidence – for example, when someone says that they feel ill. Instead, the 'status' of the body is measured by data obtained through self-tracking. The data tells one whether they are ill or not.

Referring to Marx's fetish concept,[6] the individual submits to the metric power of digital devices in order to become more efficient and to optimize their abilities and competencies. From this point of view, self-tracking can be seen as an expression of neoliberal entrepreneurship and self-maximization. The digital device becomes an Erzieher, evaluates the user and "tells" them, where they are located in relation to the (Erziehungs-)Goal.

Within self-tracking, the principle of capitalist competition is also promoted. Self-tracking apps allow individuals to challenge each other – for example, to run faster, lose more weight, or do more sports than others. Within the self-tracking culture, communication is defined by a competitive relationship between the communication partners. In the era of mobile Internet and post-digitality, social influencing, the selfie culture, and the practice of self-tracking continue the neoliberal communication practices developed in the Web 2.0 phase. This subjection of the individual under neoliberal parameters is confronted with the digital counterpublic which is a central part of the history of the Internet.

5.7 Digital Counterpublic

With the emergence of the Internet, there is also the hope of a new medium for counter-publicity or even of a counter-medium.

The Internet also grew out of the university during the sixties and seventies, whose resistance culture developed in student protests. Against the background of these cultural roots of the Internet, it is not surprising that the Internet is also addressed as a space of freedom. In the 1980s, this idea of freedom lived in hacker culture. The "Hacker Manifesto" of The Mentor can be read as an expression of this idea of freedom. In the 1990s, this idea was carried forward by net and cyberutopists. Cyberspace was understood as a post-national space – a space that knows no borders and national identities. Here, the "Declaration of Independence of the Internet," published by Jim Barlow in 1996, can be identified as a paradigmatic example.

This juxtaposition of 'cyberspace' on the one hand and 'material-physical world' on the other lives on today in the juxtaposition of 'free dark web' and 'supervised clear web.' In the 2000s, the hacktivists replaced the cyberutopists of the 1990s.

Hacktivism is a combination of the words hacker and activism. In hacktivism, strategies and techniques of hacking are explicitly used for political purposes – for example, when messages are left behind on symbolic, highly-frequented websites. Cyberguerillas like Anonymous but also counterpublic media such as Wikileaks are in the tradition of the critical dissenting voice, which is part of the history of the bourgeois public sphere.

In terms of discourse analysis, the discussion about the meaning of the Internet is represented by the relationship between a book about the future of the Internet, the review of this book, and an interview conducted in the course of collecting material for the book in question. As Cypherpunk, hacker, and founder of Wikileaks, Julian Assange is asked about anonymity on the Internet in an interview in which Eric Schmidt (the former Executive Chairman and Chief Executive Officer of Google) participated. This interview provided data for the book *The New Digital Age: Reshaping the Future of People, Nations, and Business* (2013), which Schmidt published with Jared Cohen, then the Director of Google Ideas. This book deals with issues such as data security in the digital age. It argues that although access to data poses a threat to privacy, it is not really a threat in democratic states. Democratic regulation processes would correct the transgression of privacy.

> Governments operating surveillance platforms will surely violate restrictions placed on them [...] eventually, but in democratic states with properly functioning legal systems and active civil societies, those errors will be corrected whether that means penalties for perpetrators or new safeguards put into place.
>
> (Schmidt & Cohen, 2013, p. 175)

In a book review published in the New York Times, Assange criticized the book as a euphemism of a colonizing, capitalist practice of power. In doing so, Assange points to an entanglement between state control and the control of large corporations like Google, to which individuals are subject. In his book review, Assange summarizes a power practice of the control society in the digital age:

> The authors offer an expertly banalized version of tomorrow's world: the gadgetry of decades hence is predicted to be much like what we have right now – only cooler. "Progress" is driven by the inexorable spread of American consumer technology over the surface of the earth. Already, every day, another million or so Google-run mobile devices are activated. Google will interpose itself, and hence the United States government, between the communications of every human being not in China (naughty China). Commodities just become more marvelous; young, urban professionals sleep, work and shop with greater ease and comfort; democracy is insidiously subverted by technologies of surveillance, and control is enthusiastically rebranded as "participation"; and our present world order of systematized domination, intimidation and oppression continues, unmentioned, unafflicted or faintly perturbed.
>
> (Assange, 2013, para. 13)

Assange's resistance is directed against these control practices and the ideologization of surveillance. Zimmermann states "Just look at Google. If you're a standard Google user Google knows who you're communicating with, who you know, what you're researching, potentially your sexual orientation, and your religious and philosophical beliefs" (Zimmermann in Assange et al., 2012, S. 51).

Anonymity is a strategy to formulate this resistance. In doing so, Assange updates the narrative topos of anonymous freedom of movement in cyberspace, which positions itself beyond the disciplining subjectivity constraints of the material-physical world. According to Assange, the resistance is characterized by a guerrilla-like ephemeral movement strategy. Assange describes this movement strategy in the interview with Cohen and Schmidt, which they conducted with Assange in preparation for their book *The New Digital Age: Reshaping the Future of People, Nations, and Business*:

> I am always hesitant in saying that everyone should go out and become a martyr. I don't believe that. I believe the most effective activists are those that fight and run away to fight another day, not those who fight and martyr themselves. That's about judgement – when to engage in the fight and when to withdraw so as to preserve your resources for the next fight.
>
> (Assange, 2014, S. 137)

This ephemeral freedom of movement is made possible by anonymity – which, for example, hackers discursively stage using synonyms: "If you have perfect anonymity you can fight forever, yes. You don't have to run away" (ibid.). This anonymity, which Assange describes here, was elevated by cyberactivists from Anonymous to the principle of organization.

The discursive dichotomization of 'freedom space of cyberspace versus the compulsion to individualize the material–physical world' leads to a discussion of the technological dependence of the 'platonic world' of cyberspace on the material–physical world:

> The platonic nature of the internet, ideas and information flows, is de-based by its physical origins. Its foundations are fiber optic cable lines stretching across the ocean floors, satellites spinning above our heads, computer servers housed in buildings in cities from New York to Nairobi.
>
> (Assange in Assange et al., 2012, p. 2)

In this interpretation, cyberspace appears as the world of the mind, which is confronted with the violence of the powerful of the material–physical world: "Like the soldier who slew Archimedes with a mere sword, so too could an armed militia take control of the peak development of Western civilization, our platonic realm" (Assange in Assange et al., 2012, p. 2).

According to this narrative logic, the Internet's space of freedom, the world of the mind, is exposed to the threat of claims to power by the powerful in the material–physical world. Not only do they have the power of disposal over the material–physical infrastructure of the Internet, but they also threaten to gain control over the 'platonic free space' of cyberspace:

> The new world of the internet, abstracted from the old world of brute atoms, longed for independence. But states and their friends moved to control our new world – by controlling its physical underpinnings. The state, like an army around an oil well, or a customs agent extracting bribes at the border, would soon learn to leverage its control of physical space to gain control over our platonic realm.
>
> (Assange in Assange et al., 2012, S. 2)

Assange problematizes a transformation of the Internet away from a space of freedom to a surveillance society: "If we do not, the universality of the Internet will merge global humanity into one giant grid of mass surveillance and mass control" (Assange in Assange, et al., 2012, p. 6). From this perspective, a fight about the meaning of the Internet is literally raging, in which 'increased communication' faces 'increased surveillance.' "Increased communication means you have extra freedom relative to the people who are trying to control ideas and manufacture consent, and increased surveillance means just the opposite" (Assange in Assange et al., 2012, p. 21). The topoi of this debate originate from the traditional freedom semantics of the libertarian cyberspace theorists. According to this narrative, a culture of emancipation and the disciplining strategies of a control society are dichotomously opposed to each other. Holze (2017) states that there is a war on the Internet (cf. Holze, 2017, p. 96). This 'war' fights over sovereignties of interpretation and forms of legitimation. In the center of attention are questions like:

- Which data, facts, information can be evaluated as knowledge?
- When is information 'fake news'?
- Are there alternative facts? And
- are whistleblowing and sharing unauthorized data via digital platforms strategies of legitimate knowledge? Are they communication, resistance, or betrayal?

According to Holze (2017), it is therefore the fight for information and knowledge, for the sovereignty of interpretation, neutrality, and plurality, and for the socially relevant questions: How does knowledge come about? What do we accept as knowledge? Which institutions and systems are involved and, because of current social structures, legitimized to participate in the production process of knowledge? (cf. Holze, 2017, p. 96).

Another feature of digital counter-publicity is the fact that digital counter-publicity is mostly anonymous counter-publicity. Assange refers to the strategic advantage of this anonymity: "If you have perfect anonymity, you can fight forever, yes. You don't have to run away" (Assange, 2014, p. 137). The decentralized hacker movement Anonymous stages its programmatic anonymity by resorting to patterns of iconic pop culture such as the Guy Fawkes mask, which has had a rebellious semantics since the comic narrative 'V for Vendetta.' 'V' represents the resistance against the centralized government. V is determined, independent, and tech-savvy. The Guy Fawkes mask becomes the symbol of the anonymous collectivity of the digital age. The digital anonymous collectivity radicalizes the anonymity of the critic, to whom the philosopher Fichte already had recourse. Due to the decentralized structure of the Internet, a 'critical collectivity in the net' (Wiedemann, 2018) can form that knows no leader. Thus a swarm-like 'cyberguerilla' emerges. In the sense of an interim conclusion, it can be stated that the digital counterpublic as an anonymous collective takes on the form of a digital swarm. In contrast to the masses, the digital swarm is not coherent in itself. The infrastructure forms the decentralized Internet as a meta-organization of digital networks. Networks are characterized by the fact that they can be reconfigured. This infrastructure enables the spontaneity of the digital swarm; the digital swarm is defined by "fleeting patterns that do not exhibit a fixed formation (Han, 2013, p. 22, translation by David Kergel). This swarm-shaped spontaneity is not only found in the digital counterpublic, but is also to be understood as a characteristic of the digital media structure which shapes learning in the digital age.

5.8 Digital learning and digital knowledge

Learning with digital media and learning in the digital age is a swarm-like, collaborative, and decentralized learning. In the book culture of the Gutenberg Galaxies, learning was unidirectional learning. The leading medium was the book. The author shared knowledge; the reader received knowledge. This form of knowledge transfer also shaped the electronic age. The consumer culture, as well as the advertising industry of Fordism and post-Fordism, created forms of informal-accidental learning. This informal-accidental learning was conveyed through the unidirectional mass media of the electronic age. Informal-accidental learning is, therefore, unidirectional learning. Following Baudrillard, it can be stated that unidirectional learning is non-dialogical and, thus, non-participatory learning. From the perspective of learning theory, unidirectional learning is behavioristic or cognitivist learning. In the digital age, the poly-directionality and polyphony of digital media open up the possibility of socio-constructivist, participatory learning. In order to support this thesis, a media-theoretical perspective is helpful.

5.8.1 Excursus: media theory – from media to the analysis of media structures

Media theoretical reflections analyze the structure of media on a theoretical level. One goal of media-theoretical research is the analysis of media, their structures, and their effects on the self/world relations of subjects. A media-theoretical analysis faces the task of defining the term 'medium' more precisely. Three levels of concepts can be identified here.

- On the one hand, there is a 'common sense' understanding of (mass) media. This common-sense understanding can also be seen in the 'everyday media concept.' Outside academic contexts, the question "What is media?" will not pose problems. The answer would be radio, television, and newspapers. Referring to these leading media of the urban modernity and the electronic age, one sometimes speaks of a 'narrow concept of media' (cf. Lagaay & Lauer, 2004). This 'narrow concept of media' is opposed by a 'broad concept of media.'
- In the course of the discussions, which – at least implicitly – assume a broad concept of media, a traditional definition of the medium is adopted. In this traditional understanding of the medium, the term "medium" is used as a means, a mediator, or something mediating. In addition to the sender and receiver, the medium assumes the function of a mediator as 'the third' in the communication process. The medium carries the information and transmits the information. According to the latter concept, a clear distinction is made between information and medium which conveys the information.

- This clear distinction between content from the medium as mediator and information as the content is questioned by representatives of a 'wide concept of media.' McLuhan's statement that "the Media is the Message" is probably the most popular in this context (cf. McLuhan, 1964). The medium is not a phenomenon in itself that unrecognizably conveys media content or information in the communication process. Instead, media content and media form cannot be separated from each other.

- From this perspective – and this can be identified as the primary position of a broad understanding of media – a medium is never neutral, but constitutes the content. When a Shakespearean play is seen in the theatre, the impression, experience, and phenomenal structure of the play and its content are different than when the play is received as an audiobook or viewed as a film. The play as such exists in the performative (re)production, which is bound to the medium. Based on this example, it can be stated that media form and media content are inextricably linked with each other. This dialectical interplay of media content and media form makes it difficult to identify precisely what a medium is. In the following, a media-theoretical reading is proposed that refers to praxeological approaches.

Media is not the subject of research. Instead, medial structures become the focus of reflection. In other words, the way in which information is conveyed and the way in which people interact with each other can also be analyzed as the medial structure of (social) phenomena. The media structure can be analyzed as the way in which the potential for interaction is opened up by a phenomenon. For example, television has a unidirectional media structure. Television enables only one way of communication, in which there is a transmitter directed at a mass of receivers. Television, therefore, has a unidirectional media structure and cannot be used in any other way. Conversely, Web 2.0 media of the internet has a poly-directional structure. Each actor can become a sender and receiver at any time and can send a potentially unlimited amount of information to other actors as well as receive a potentially unlimited amount of information.

The approach to carry out media-theoretical analyses as an analysis of media structures is in the tradition of praxeological analyses, or the so-called 'Practice Turn' (cf. Reckwitz, 2003). The 'Practice Turn' describes a practice-theoretical orientation that focuses on the 'doing' of something. Every social reality must first and foremost be socially produced. The medial structure is produced in interactions. The content "You look good today" unfolds a different meaning depending on the respective form in which it manifests. As a personal face-to-face greeting, it acquires a different meaning than via a telephone conversation, or as an utterance in a letter, or when a host greets his television viewers via the camera with the words "You look good today." Through the content-form dynamic, the meanings of phenomena unfold.

The medial structure of a phenomenon is created in the practice of social interactions and consequently unfolds in interaction processes. From a media-theoretical perspective, these interaction processes can also be analyzed as processes of medialization.

The analysis of medial structures is often complicated by the "paradox of the medial" (Mersch, 2006, p. 226). With the analytical focus on content, the medial structure of a phenomenon 'disappears.' We often only become aware of the mobile phone as a mediator when a 'lousy connection' limits the quality of the conversation. At this moment, we perceive the media structure of the mobile phone, which enables us to communicate 'remotely, 'We can listen to our conversation partner as though very close to us, even though they could physically be thousands of kilometers away. The analysis of the medial structure of phenomena has to face the challenge of

- identifying the 'content/form' dynamics of interaction processes and thus
- decoding the medial structure of social phenomena.

Hierarchies and dependencies are also embedded in the 'content/form' dynamics of interaction events. Baudrillard's analysis of television and radio as mass media of the electronic age is an example of this.

Baudrillard's analyses take place during the electronic age in which the unidirectional orientation of mass media dominates. With the internet, media structures are established, which, in Baudrillard's sense, enable dialogical interaction-processes. In the course of the constitution of the digital age, a dialogical modification of the medial structure can be observed. With the establishment of Web 2.0, digitally-supported dialogical communication possibilities increasingly establish themselves. The participatory media structures that define Web 2.0 as a so-called 'participatory network' require dialogical communication so that the participatory media potential can be appropriately realized – for example, Wikipedia cannot unfold without a dialogue. At this point, it is worth taking a media-theoretically informed look at the media structure of digital communication.

5.8.2 From digital poly-directional and polyphonic medial-structure to digital knowledge

The communication processes via the internet are digitally-based and require a transfer into digital codes. Digitization forms the media structure of digital communication. In contrast to the media of book culture (books, newspapers) or the electronic age (radio, television), the media structure of the digital is defined by the fact that it possesses the computer as its technical core; media content is conveyed through computational processes and in the course of this is also shaped and changed (*cf.* Zorn, 2011, p. 176). The representation of media content is the result of calculations that are carried out again and again when digital content is created or called up.

Digitized content is displayed on digital media or digital end devices such as tablets, smartphones, or laptops. Digital media are involved in the production of media content as information-transmitting instances (*cf.* Schelhowe, 2007, p. 46). Digital media contents are produced again and again in the process of transmitting the information via digitization. Unlike a book that has been printed and is thus a final medium, digital media contents are more a process than a product (cf. Schelhowe, 2007, p. 47). If you look for a book, you know where it is on the shelf and which page to open in order to read a passage. This media content had been printed, sold/bought and put on the shelf. Unlike the book on the shelf, digital media content is either there or not. The present is a characteristic of media content. The content to be conveyed in the process of information exchange appears immediately on the digital device. That can be analyzed as the implosion of time and place via the internet: there is no shelf, but the content appears on your device.

From a praxeological perspective, the knowledge that emerges in the context of Web 2.0 applications such as wikis can be characterized as a result of interactions. Within these interactions, new media content is constantly produced. Herein lies a dialogical dimension that characterizes the media structure of the digital. This dialogical dimension of the media structure of the digital is represented in so-called 'User Generated Content.' Through the technical possibilities of digital communication, consumers can become producers of web content (*cf.* Gaiser, 2008). The Web 2.0 phase is a communication platform on which users can actively shape and create content. While unidirectional media send information in one direction, the internet is characterized by a poly-directional and polyphonic structure. Potentially, people can connect with each other in a dialogue. It is possible to communicate in all directions. Instead of 'one voice' broadcasting, as is the case with television and radio, all actors potentially have a voice.

The structure of 'digital knowledge' can be derived on the basis of the media structure of digital. Digital knowledge is based on dialogic-collaborative communication processes. In the course of these dialogic-collaborative communication processes, poly-directional and polyphonic knowledge is constructed. Wikipedia is an ideal example of digital knowledge. Wikis make it possible to adequately depict the dynamics of collective knowledge production and the incompleteness of digital knowledge since the articles can always be revised.

At the same time, Wikipedia shows how much digital knowledge lies in the tradition of the Enlightenment, and thus part of civil society and the civic public. Wikipedia is an online encyclopedia in the tradition of the *Encyclopédie ou Dictionnaire raisonné des sciences, des arts et des métiers* (1751–1780). The *Encyclopédie* and Wikipedia systematically present knowledge for a better understanding of the world, a crucial feature of the Enlightenment. *Encyclopédie* and

Wikipedia are projects that represent collective achievements. Diderot, who initiated the *Encyclopédie*, understood this project as a collective undertaking:

> When one considers the immense material for an encyclopedia, the only thing one perceives distinctly is that it cannot be the work of a single man. How could a single man, in the short span of his life, manage to comprehend and develop the universal system of nature and art? Whereas the numerous scientific community of La Crusca spent forty years constituting its vocabulary, and whereas our French Academicians had labored for sixty years on their dictionary, before producing its first edition! Yet what is the dictionary of a language? What is a lexicon, even executed as well as it can be? A precise collection of the articles to be filled in by an encyclopedic and analytical dictionary.
>
> (Diderot, without year, para. 4)[7]

The media structure of the digital enables the collective character of knowledge generation to a higher extent than was possible at the time of the *Encyclopédie*. Wikis open up space for a dialogic-collaborative production of knowledge that reflects the ideal of the Enlightenment. By participating in Wikipedia as a form of the public sphere, the individuum can enlighten itself through discursive knowledge production. This self-enlightenment makes it possible for individuals to escape a self-inflicted immaturity. If one follows these considerations, digital knowledge construction and its dialogic-collaborative structure can be understood as part of the bourgeois public sphere in the digital age. The characteristics of digital knowledge also shape learning in the digital age. For instance, the ephemeral structure of digital knowledge is always in motion, and can be understood as fluid learning. This fluid learning as digital learning or learning in the digital age is signified with the term 'e-learning.'

5.8.3 The unfolding of e-learning as fluid learning in the digital age

E-learning signifies teaching and learning in the digital age. Accordingly, e-learning is a manifestation of the media change of digitization in the pedagogical field. In other words, e-learning is the effect of digitization in the context of teaching and learning. It is not surprising that e-learning also raises questions about the media dimension of learning.

The media structure of the digital inscribes itself in didactic strategies. Sharples et al. (2005) developed a parallelization of a 'new' learner-centered understanding of learning and 'new' technologies. This parallelization represents the impact of media structures on pedagogical aspect. Participatory learning strategies find their medial equivalent in the participative, poly-directional structure of digital media (Table 5.1).

Table 5.1 Convergence between learning and technology (own figure according to Sharples et al., 2005, p. 4)

New Learning	New Technology
Personalized	Personal
Learner-centered	User-centered
Situated	Mobile
Collaborative	Networked
Ubiquitous	Ubiquitous
Lifelong	Durable

Digital knowledge is also hypertextual, associative knowledge. Learning takes place based on decentralized networking through polyphonic and poly-directional communication. Thus, digital knowledge stands in contrast to the linear knowledge of book culture and the electronic age. Although the media structures for the construction of digital knowledge did not exist on a broad scale until the early 2000s, the discussion focuses on the advantages of digital knowledge over linear knowledge tradition.

In addition to dialogical potential, the decentralized, hypertextual structure of the internet is a characteristic of online-based teaching and learning – and digital knowledge in general. In this context, hypertext can be understood as a web-like structure that links information/objects with each other through hyperlinks (hypertext nodes). The hypertext enables non-linear 'jumps' between the references (*cf.* Kirpal & Vogel, 2016, p. 143). These jumps can quickly be executed via a computer. At the media level, the phenomenon of the hypertext is related to the associative structure of digital knowledge.

The non-linear and multi-modal structure of the hypertext becomes the medial representative of a non-linear, associative way of thinking. The modern roots of hypertextual thinking lie among others with Vannevar Bush, an advisor to the then US President Roosevelt.

In 1945, Bush designed the model of a Memex machine (Memory Extended), which anticipated hypertext structures as a form of the analog computer and with reference to the state of research at the time. Bush presented this model in the article "As we may think," which appeared in the magazine *The Atlantic Monthly*. The Memex is a machine conceived by Bush with which knowledge can be collected and organized: "A memex is a device in which an individual stores all his books, records, and communications, and which is mechanized so that it may be consulted with exceeding speed and flexibility" (Bush, 1945, S. 121). The Memex should enable an associative form of knowledge organization. "It affords an immediate step, however, to associative indexing, the basic idea of which is a provision whereby any item may be caused at will to select immediately and automatically another" (Bush, 1945, S. 123). According to Bush, this form of associative indexation corresponds to the human knowledge structure.

The real heart of the matter of selection, however, goes deeper than a lag in the adoption of mechanisms by libraries, or a lack of development of devices for their use. Our ineptitude in getting at the record is largely caused by the artificiality of systems of indexing. When data of any sort are placed in storage, they are filed alphabetically or numerically and information is found (when it is) by tracing it down from subclass to subclass. It can be in only one place, unless duplicates are used; one has to have rules as to which path will locate it, and the rules are cumbersome. Having found one item, moreover, one has to emerge from the system and re-enter on a new path. The human mind does not work that way. It operates by association. With one item in its grasp, it snaps instantly to the next that is suggested by the association of thoughts, in accordance with some intricate web of trails carried by the cells of the brain. It has other characteristics, of course; trails that are not frequently followed are prone to fade, items are not fully permanent, memory is transitory. Yet the speed of action, the intricacy of trails, the detail of mental pictures, is awe-inspiring beyond all else in nature.

(Bush, 1945, S. 121)

The Memex machine already prepares the image of the desktop PC. The work table was the basis of the PC and later replaced by mobile digital devices such as smartphones, tablets, or wearables. Bush prepared an interpretation of hypertextual thinking, which largely shapes current e-learning concepts such as e-learning 2.0 or mobile learning. The dimension of associative, decentral thinking is also represented in the concept of the hypertext. The term hypertext was established by Ted Nelson in the 1960s:

Let me introduce the word "hypertext" to mean a body of written or pictorial material interconnected in such a complex way, that it could not conveniently be presented or represented on paper. It may contain summaries, or maps of list contents and their interrelations; it may contain annotations, additions and footnotes from scholars who have examined it.

(Nelson, 1965, S. 96)

Nelson founded the Xanadu project in 1960. It was named after a place where Kubla Khan had a pleasure palace built. The Xanadu project envisaged a decentralized storage project. In the sense of a universal library, documents were to be linked associatively. Although the Xanadu project failed due to the complexity of the project, Nelson's attempt to adopt a technical infrastructure to the decentralized, non-linear structure of knowledge organization prepares innovative forms of e-learning as developed in the course of e-Learning 2.0.

In 2004, George Siemens finally developed the Connectivism concept which he understands as a learning theory of the digital age. Siemens' approach follows the tradition of conceptualizing non-linear, associative thinking. Based on this non-linear, associative thinking, digital knowledge is generated. This digital knowledge and digital learning needs a new, appropriate learning theory.

Behaviorism, cognitivism, and (socio-)constructivism were all developed before the digital age. Can these 'pre-digital' learning theories adequately model learning in the digital age? If one asks Siemens, the answer is clearly "no!" Siemens does not leave it at 'no,' but provides in 'connectivism' a model that claims to be a learning theory for the digital age. Siemens' consideration is that the learning opportunities that result from the internet cannot be worked up by 'classical learning theories' such as behaviorism, cognitivism, and (socio-)constructivism. It is, therefore, necessary to formulate a learning theory for the digital age:

> Behaviorism, cognitivism, and constructivism are the three broad learning theories most often utilized in the creation of instructional environments. These theories, however, were developed in a time, when learning was not impacted through technology. Over the last twenty years, technology has reorganized how we live, how we communicate, and how we learn. Learning needs and theories, that describe learning principles and processes, should be reflective of underlying social environments.
>
> (Siemens, 2004, para. 1)

According to Siemens, connectivism makes it possible to describe interaction and learning processes made possible by the internet from a learning-theoretical perspective. One focus of connectivism is, therefore, the decentralized possibilities that the internet opens up for learning contexts. "Knowledge, that resides in a database, needs to be connected with the right people in the right context in order to be classified as learning" (Siemens, 2004, S. 5).

The basic idea is that learners dock or connect to digital learning communities (e.g., in wikis, MOOCs, chat rooms, etc.) according to their learning needs: "In Connectivism, learning occurs when a learner connects to a learning community and feeds information into it" (Şahin, 2012, p. 442). The learning process arises through the active establishment of links between content, technical, and social resources. Ravenscroft (2011) sees here structural equality between the media structure of the internet and the form of decentralized, self-directed learning of connectivism:

> But this is precisely where there is a harmonious join because connectivism, with its deliberate focus on the here-and-now reality of how digital networks support new forms of connections, social relations, and dialogue, provides a sociotechnical frame or set of creative constraints within which contemporary social constructivist activities occur.
>
> (Ravenscroft, 2011, S. 144)

Ravenscroft's 'socio-technical' description of learning combines the many-to-many structure of the internet with flexible learning strategies.

Connectivist learning is social learning and a dialogical process. From this perspective, connectivism is in the tradition of the mash-up culture of the internet. The remix and mashup culture of the internet is an effect of the decentralized, poly-directional, and polyphonic socio-technical structure of the internet.

> Technology could enable a whole generation to create – remixed films, new forms of music, digital art, a new kind of storytelling, writing, a new technology for poetry, criticism, political activism – and then, through infrastructure of the Internet, share creativity with others.
>
> (Lessig, 2001, S. 9)

It is precisely this ephemeral, fluid, non-linear, and non-static form of communication, in which content is produced and changed by users, that poses a challenge to media literacy in the digital age. Thus, according to Weel, a central challenge lies in conveying strategies to confidently "deal with turning the solid, unchangeable monuments of print into the continual, ever-changing events of the digital realm" (Weel, 2011, S. 218). The changes in media possibilities and social relationships, therefore, pose a challenge for the design of teaching/learning scenarios.

From an e-didactic perspective, the challenge is to develop strategies that enable learning that is adequate to the structures of digital communication and digital knowledge. Particular care must be taken to ensure that the dialogical and collaborative potential of the digital is appropriately updated in teaching/learning scenarios. The differentiation between cooperative and collaborative forms of work for e-didactic planning appears to be an essential distinction.

- Cooperative work is entirely in the tradition of Fordist work: the individual parts of the task are worked on by individual learners and finally joined together. Experience has shown that this strategy is often used in group presentations and other group work by learners. Although this seems efficient, it often diminishes the results, since there is no dialogical validation of the work results.
- In collaborative work, a dialogical discussion takes place at each step. Dialogical cooperation, in particular, usually leads to high-quality work results and also increases the quality of the learning experience (cf. Kergel & Heidkamp, 2015). Dialogical cooperation can be realized via digital media in a low-threshold and flexible manner, independent of time and place.

Collaborative forms of learning are becoming increasingly popular methods of adult education, because they involve all students in the process of learning. Social software is based heavily on participation, and this is apparent in a number of features including tagging, voting, versioning, hyperlinking, and searching, as well as discussion and commenting. The power of this kind of software is that it includes all in the process of creating group-based collections of knowledge and artifacts, that are of specific interest to the learning community (Wheeler, 2008, S. 5).

5.8.4 From collective authorship to the common creative license

Wikipedia articles are created through collective writing; knowledge is generated and validated collaboratively. Wikipedia articles can also be understood as scientific narratives because they order realities in a meaningful way and validate them intersubjectively. By allowing entries to be discussed and changed at any time, the space of ephemeral collaborative knowledge construction is opened up. Due to its participative approach, this form of collaborative knowledge generation de-finishes the author/reader relationship. Analogous to the implosion of time and space via digital media, Web 2.0 opens an implosion of the relation author/reader: the recipient and the producer of content coincide. "Moreover, the 'democratization' of textual production, distribution and consumption creates an entirely new relationship between author and reader" (Weel, 2011, p. 5).

Lessig (2009), a co-founder of the Creative Commons Initiative, notes that a 'Read and Write Culture' has established itself in the digital age, which distinguishes itself explicitly from the 'Read Only Culture.' This Read and Write Culture constitutes a textual instability (*cf.* Weel, 2011) that corresponds to the ephemeral structure of the cultures of the digital. "The printing press has in the course of time created a (largely unconscious) expectation of stability and permanence of form and content" (Weel, 2011, p. 149). The participatory possibilities of Web 2.0 set this text in motion. "Different people can comment on same digital text, giving rise to, for example, various – virtual – combinations of texts and commentaries" (Weel, 2011, p. 158). The text unfolds in a 'web' of reception and commentary. At the latest in the act of commenting, the text undergoes a remix. Each reader/author is an element of this text. A text can be received and commented on/remixed by several readers. The Remix Culture reproduces a textual instability performatively. The text also makes the author 'unstable.'

Against the background of these considerations, the concept of the author can be replaced accordingly by the concept of collective authorship. Collective authorship refers to the possibilities of collaborative knowledge production and at the same time, means a farewell to the figure of the author of the book culture of the Gutenberg Galaxy. Instead of hierarchical relations between author and reader, which is constituted by the unidirectional structure of the book, the medial structure of Web 2.0 enables dialogue-based collective authorship. Such collective authorship can also be understood as postmodern authorship since the text is successively generated through critical reflection and a dialogical relationship with one another.

The Creative Common Licenses represent the media–related shifts in the bourgeois concept of the author.

In 2001 the organization Creative Commons was founded in the USA, and a license model was developed which was made publicly available. This license model allows the author to grant other users low-threshold usage rights to his work. The granting of rights of use also allows the author to explicitly agree that the content they generated be edited and become part of new works. Through Creative Common Licensing, the work becomes a free content, so that free use and further distribution of the content is possible under copyright law. The development of free content represents an approach that originates from the Open Resource movement, which was constituted in the course of internet development.

The starting point of the Open Source or Free Software movement was initially to program a competitive and better operating system as an alternative to the products of commercial providers (above all Microsoft). Instead of the source code being written and further developed by a few programmers, software should be developed in an open and collaborative manner (*cf.* Brandt, 2009). With reference to the Open Source movement, collective authorship can be understood as part of early internet culture. In the 1980s, the 'GNU General Public License' (GNU GPL) was developed as general permission to publish. The GNU GPL raises the idea of free software to the level of copyright licensing. With the GNU GPL, users are granted the right to copy, edit, and make publicly available the software in question, free of royalties.

The Creative Commons license model follows the tradition of the Open Source approach and the GNU GPL model. While the Open Source approach is defined by the fact that the source code of a software is freely accessible and can be further developed, Creative Common licenses allow similar dynamics in the field of text, video, and image processing. Source Open stands for a range of licenses for software with the commonality that the source code is publicly available. The requirements of open source software go beyond the readability/availability of the source code since the exchange of ideas for the further development of the software is an intended objective underlying the opening of the source code. The Creative Commons Model continues this idea and transfers it to knowledge products/formations beyond software development. Over the years, the Creative Commons license model has been continuously developed, so that version 3.0 is currently available. This license model, in turn, has six sublicenses, which makes it possible to change the terms of use gradually. The gradation of the conditions of use ranges from a prescribed unchangeable passing on of the contents up to the granting of the possibility that contents may be further processed and/or changed. In general, within the framework of this licensing model, the author remains the legal reference person, since they must state their name as licensor. This is marked with the name CC BY, which is obligatory for every form of licensing, according to Creative Commons. The Creative Commons licenses can be generated via the Creative Commons Initiative website with a few clicks. Under the Creative Commons licensing model, the author can prohibit his work from being edited, remixed, and then republished: CC BY-ND (ND stands for Non Derivation). It is also possible to have a distribution under the same conditions that you grant yourself: CC BY-SA. Here SA stands for Share Alike. If, for example, a work is available free of charge, the following conditions apply: with the CC0 (Public Domain Dedication) license, licensors can waive all rights or grant an unrestricted license. A work can then be copied, modified, distributed, or otherwise brought into the public domain. However, the legal question here is whether a work can be solved in this way by the author.

The Creative Commons licensing model can be understood as an approach to respond to the collaborative dynamics that enable digital-based forms of knowledge production. A text is no longer finitely 'fixed' but can be further-written and distributed under certain conditions of the Creative Commons License. Even if the concept of the author – a phenomenon of the Gutenberg galaxy – is not thus abolished, it is set in motion by the possibility of processing. At the level of licensing, the Creative Commons model reflects the emerging collective authorship in the digital age, which has already been hinted at semiotically in Barthes' deconstruction of the author in the electronic age. From an epistemological perspective, it can be stated that such symbolic references are made to the collaborative dimension of knowledge production and the infinite movement of knowledge or the trans-subjective dimension of knowledge generation processes.

Through its decentralized structure and dialogical orientation, the Internet provides spaces for a collaborative knowledge generation process that can lead to collaborative authorship. These possibilities must be used for learning purposes.

Notes

1 Media convergence refers to the convergence of previously separate media areas.
2 The Chicago Boys were are a group of Chilean economists, most of whom studied at the University of Chicago from 1956 to 1970. They were inspired by the ideas of Friedrich August von Hayek and Milton Friedman. Under Augusto Pinochet's rule, they became influential economically and socio-politically in Chile. The Chicago Boys were convinced of the neoliberal concept of the superiority of free markets. The free market should be established through privatization and deregulation. Because of the political conditions under the dictatorship, the Chicago Boys were initially able to implement their far-reaching reform ideas without any significant cutbacks.
3 Influencers are people who report on brands or present products in social networks. Through a high reputation and a strong presence, they have a significant

influence on their followers. Articles, videos, and photos are the most common form in which opinions about brands and products are shared.

Opinion leaders have always been important for companies and their reach. But digital media has made collaboration even more relevant. Influencers communicate via different channels and are particularly active in social networks. Communication via platforms such as Facebook, Youtube, Twitter, Snapchat, and Instagram offers the possibility to address the recipients directly.

4 https://www.bvdw.org/themen/publikationen/detail/artikel/digital-trends-umfrage-zum-umgang-mit-influencern/, last accessed: 21 April 2020.

5 DARPA is the successor organization to ARPA.

6 The fetish character denotes a quasi-religious meaning that goods "adhere to." As a "mythical character," the fetish-character is not part of the utility value of a commodity. The fetish character is the interpretation of a product, which is attributed to it, although this meaning lies outside the utility value. In other words: the fetish-character of a product designates the dimension or the value which emanates from a product and which does not result from the utility value of the product. A Gucci handbag, for example, is more than just a well-made handbag. Instead, the handbag refers to 'fashion awareness' and 'financial resources;' the wearer of a Gucci handbag has the fashion awareness and the money to afford such a handbag. To ensure that everyone perceives this, the Gucci logo is visible on Gucci products—the Gucci handbag is a socio-semiotic phenomenon. According to Marx, people create fetishes and then subordinate them to them. The fetish-character of a product is an expression of human self-submission to things he creates himself.

7 http://quod.lib.umich.edu/d/did/did2222.0000.004/--encyclopedia?rgn=main;view=fulltext;q1=diderot. Zugegriffen: 28 August 2015. Last accessed: 3 March 2020.

Chapter 6

Outlook – from Bildung and e-learning to (media) Bildung 2.0

In Bildung-Processes, everything has to be discovered, and everything has to be questioned. Bildung knows no boundaries of knowledge. It is precisely the overcoming of the limits of knowledge that can be achieved via a collaborative form of knowledge construction. The Bildung-Characteristic of explorative curiosity requires a different way of thinking and thus requires dialogue partners. From this perspective, Bildung appears as a prosocial, collaborative learning process, which is inter-individually coined by the Bildung-Characteristics explorative curiosity and self-efficacy.

The dialogical communication structure of Bildung enables the exploration of other ways of thinking. The subject in its process of becoming unfolds within in dialogic-collaborative contexts on the basis of the dialogical communication. From this perspective, education is also a prosocial, collaborative process.

Since the beginning of the 2000s and the dawn of the digital age, many e-tools have been developed that promote collaborative learning at the media level. For example, many of the popular social web applications enable collaborative writing. Seen from the perspective of the unfolding of e-learning, the development of these tools falls into the phase of "e-Learning 2.0." In order to adequately present the concept of e-Learning 2.0, a brief description of the development of e-learning is relevant.

6.1 The becoming of e-learning

In addition to media theoretical analysis, there is also a genealogical perspective of analysis. The genealogical perspective reconstructs the emergence of e-learning as an effect of the Internet's development. With the establishment of the digital age, a new form of learning is also developing: Information and Communication (ICT)-enabled education or, more precisely, e-learning.

Although e-learning, as such, emerged with the global establishment of the Internet, e-learning has its roots in the so-called machine-supported learning and programmed learning, which stands in the behaviorist tradition. Instructional programs controlled learning, whereby the subject matter has been broken down into learning tasks. Once a task has been successfully completed, the next task is presented to the learner. The role of the teacher was largely filled by teaching programs. A first intensive theoretical discussion about the link of teaching/learning and machines took place in the 1960s, a time in which cybernetic models and cognitivist learning concepts increasingly unfolded (cf. Kergel, 2014). With the beginning of the 'PC Era' in the 1980s, computer-aided learning experienced a renewed surge in popularity. Computer-based training (CBT) was offered in the form of teaching and learning programs, particularly in-company training. CBT included teaching programs that could be accessed via CD-Rom or that are stored directly on the computer. Until the end of the 1990s, CBT was the most widespread form of e-learning avant la lettre. With the establishment of the Internet, web-based training (WBT) has been added. WBT comprises all teaching programs that are accessible via the Internet. With e-Learning 1.0, e-learning as we know it finally saw the light of day at the end of the 1990s. E-Learning 1.0 was followed at relatively short intervals by e-Learning 2.0 and post-digital, mobile learning. All three phases are briefly outlined below:

- **E-Learning 1.0**: Although computer-based learning already existed before the Internet, e-learning gained the importance it has today through the commercial opening and the global and mass dissemination of the Internet. The term e-learning thus increasingly established itself from the mid-1990s onwards – at a time when Amazon (1995), Netflix (1996), and Google (1998) were central players in the 'digital economy.' Initially, e-learning was oriented towards conventional forms of learning. In universities, for example, so-called learning management systems were set up, for example, Moodle and Blackboard. At the beginning of the 2000s, a digital-supported learning or rudimentary form of e-learning was established, at least basically, in the field of higher education – a development step from which German schools are still a long way off.
- **E-Learning 2.0 – The digital 'shift from teaching to learning'**: With the essays "Connectivism" (2004) by George Siemens and "E-learning 2.0" (2005) by Stephen Downes, an e-didactic paradigm was increasingly established which defines itself by transferring the collaborative potentials of 'Web 2.0' into the field of teaching/learning. Web 2.0 (cf. O'Reilly, 2006) enables the 'consumer' to become the 'producer' of web content through technical innovations (cf. Gaiser, 2008). The user becomes the 'prosumer.' The Internet increasingly offered the possibility of being used as a communication platform. In the e-didactic discourse, the extended freedom of action in the digital domain is discussed above all through a critical valuation of learning management systems such as Moodle. Learning management systems were considered 'walled gardens' which only enable an 'island-like e-learning' that takes place within the garden walls. The actual Internet and the actual possibilities of learning wait next door (cf. Ehlers, 2011, p. 59).

In the future it will be more widely recognized that the learning comes not from the design of learning content but in how it is used. Most e-learning theorists are already there and are exploring how learning content – whether professionally authored or created by students – can be used as the basis for learning activities rather than the conduit for learning content (Downes, 2005, para. 37).

- Didactic approaches of e-Learning 2.0 emphasized situational, self-organized learning, which should be realized in the authentic world of the Internet and not within the walls of a learning management systems. Instead of a central learning platform, individual applications such as blogs should become individual learning platforms. Due to the poly-directional and polyphonic potential of Web 2.0 media, the learners can network or 'connect' to each other for socio-collaborative learning processes. From this perspective, learning managements systems, which makes e-Learning 1.0 possible, would be replaced by individual learning platforms, which enables individual, flexible learning within the socio-collaborative contexts of the Web 2.0.
- **Mobile learning as post-digital (e-)learning:** Mobile learning is increasingly establishing and based on the spread of mobile Internet. With mobile Internet, digital communication has inscribed itself in our everyday lives. The ubiquity of the Internet in social practice means that digital communication is an integral part of our lifeworld. The digital is so absorbed in our living world that we can consider ourselves to have reached a state of the 'post-digital.' The digitally mediated virtual world of the Internet and the material-physical world are inseparably intertwined. Accordingly, there is no digital learning on the one hand and mobile learning on the other. This is what the term 'mobile learning' stands for, which is not interpreted as a variant of e-learning, but as a form of learning of the post-digital age. Despite this demarcation, mobile learning adopts the socio-constructivist foundation of e-learning 2.0.

The polyphonic as well as poly-directional oriented strategies of the Web 2.0 can be brought together with the normative, dialogical approach of Bildung.

Since Web 2.0, poly-directional and polyphonic communication possibilities have increasingly existed. Based on Bildung-Theoretical considerations, cornerstones for normative, well-founded e-learning can be conceptualized.

6.2 Bildungs-ethics and quality management of teaching and learning (in the digital age)

The approach of Bildung-Ethics does not claim to develop a comprehensive pedagogical ethic. Instead, Bildung-Theory focuses on a normative-knowledge theoretical approach that is of central importance for pedagogical theory and practice. The term 'Bildung-Ethics' refers to the framing of Bildung according to ethical aspects and is based on the premise that the subject develops in and with society.

Bildung-Ethics focuses on the dimensions of social practices in which the actors involved can develop a self/world relationship based on the Bildung-Characteristics, explorative curiosity and expectations of self-efficacy. In other words, Bildung possesses an ethical dimension. Bildung-Ethics can be defined as an ethically grounded epistemological process in which the subject gains knowledge about themself and the world and thus forms a self/world relationship. This ethically grounded epistemological process can be defined as Bildung. Bildung-Ethics stress the responsibility that the counterpart as the Other in the learning process of Bildung 'develops' the Bildung-Characteristics explorative curiosity and expectations of self-efficacy. In the sense of empirically applied ethics research, it has to be evaluated whether the way individuals assume responsibility for others is within pedagogical contexts (cf. also empirically Kergel, 2018). According to the concept of Bildung-Ethics, mutual responsibility in pedagogical contexts are set in relation to the aforementioned Bildung-Characteristics.

On the basis of these considerations, the normative dimension of Bildung provides the epistemological foundation for a high-quality teaching and learning (in the digital age).

Quality is increasingly becoming a leading concept in pedagogical discourses. Concerning the pedagogical field, it should be noted that there is no final definition of which characteristics define the quality of education and learning processes. One consequence of determining quality in the pedagogical field is to derive process-specific quality parameters. In other words: Quality – defined as the appropriateness of purpose – is contextual and dependent on the objective of the respective pedagogical process. Evaluating the quality of learning and teaching processes requires the identification of setting targets and objectives which are adapted to the respective pedagogical process. Quality parameters can then be derived from these target settings/objectives. In other words, the formulation of quality is a question of definition. It must be considered what is appropriate, why it is appropriate, and in which pedagogical contexts it is appropriate. This approach leads directly from the quality to the evaluation as a crucial part of quality management.

Evaluation is characterized by checking the existence of quality characteristics. In order to achieve this, indicators must be identified that refer to the existence of quality criteria. If the definition of a quality term has been provided, and quality indicators are identified, scientific data collection procedures and evaluation strategies can be used to examine to what extent the pedagogical process matches the quality criteria. Considerations can follow this as to which measures can bring the 'actual value' closer to the 'target value.' This evaluation process can be visualized schematically as a circle (Figure 6.1).

A Bildung-oriented evaluation is characterized by the fact that the development of Bildung is set as a target value. In the course of a Bildung-oriented evaluation, it has to be assessed whether or not the pedagogical processes to

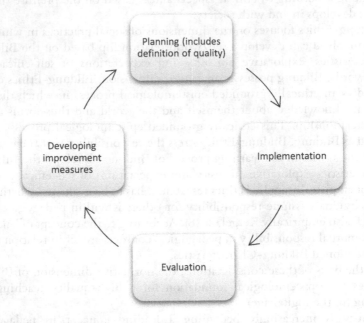

Figure 6.1 Quality definition, and the finding of suitable indicators represent a theory-practice transfer that raises the question of the measurability of quality characteristics (own illustration).

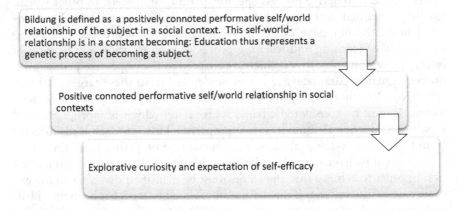

Figure 6.2 The scheme illustrates the process of a Bildung-orientated evaluation (own illustration).

be evaluated fulfill the Bildung-Characteristics. In other words, the Bildung-Characteristics become quality-characteristics through a Bildung-oriented evaluation. This is a starting point for defining the quality concept of an education-oriented evaluation approach. The criteria that define Bildung-oriented didactics can be used here as indicators. Transferred to the concept of quality in a Bildung-oriented evaluation, it is possible to concretize the evaluation scheme as follows (Figure 6.2).

A Bildung-oriented quality concept enables the normative foundation of innovative forms of digital-based learning, such as e-Learning 2.0 or mobile learning. Based on a Bildung-oriented concept of quality, digital learning, despite all disruptive dynamics, stands in the tradition of civil society. The values of enlightenment, self-determination, the critique of knowledge, and the critique of power are thus transferred into the digital age. The motion of learning in the digital age moves between Bildung-Tradition, the technical, and – today especially – digital innovation.

Bibliography

Ades, D. (1975). *Dada und Surrealismus*. München: Knaur.

Alves, A. (2019). *The German Tradition of Self-Cultivation (Bildung) and Its Historical Meaning*. http://orcid.org/0000-0002-0810-650X

Ambrosius, L. E. (2007). *Woodrow Wilson and the Birth of a Nation: American Democracy and International Relations*. doi: 10.1080/09592290701807168.

Andrejevic, M. (2005). The Work of Watching One Another: Lateral Surveillance, Risk, and Governance. In *Surveillance & Society* 2(4), 479–497.

Assange, J. (2013). *The Banality of Don't be Evil*. URL: http://www.nytimes.com/2013/06/02/opinion/sunday/the-banality-of-googles-dont-be-evil.html. Zuletzt zugegriffen: 13 Oktober 2017.

Assange, J. (2014). *When Wikileaks Meets Google*. New York: Or Books.

Assange, J., Appelbaum, J., Müller-Maghun, A., & Zimmermann, A. (2012). *Cypherpunks. Freedom and the Future of the Internet*. New York: Or Books.

Apple, M. W. (2006). *Educating the 'Right Way'. Markets, Standards, God, and Inequality*. New York: Routledge.

Aronowitz, S., & Giroux, H. A. (1991). *Postmodern Education: Politics, Culture, and Social*. Minneapolis: University of Minnesota Press.

Aufderheide, P., & Firestone, C. M. (1993). *Media Literacy: A Report of the National Leadership Conference on Media Literacy*. Washington, DC: Aspen Institute.

Baacke, D. (2007). *Medienpädagogik*. Tübingen: De Gruyter.

Bainbridge, J. (2010) *The Rise of the Action Figure and the Changing Face of 'children's' Entertainment*. doi: 10.1080/10304312.2010.510592.

Bak, M. P., & Kessler, T. (2012). Mir gefällt's, wenn's euch gefällt! Konformitätseffekte bei Facebook. In *Journal of Business and Media Psychology* 3(2), 23–30.

Ball, H. (1916). Dada Manifesto. URL: https://www.wired.com/beyond-the-beyond/2016/07/hugo-balls-dada-manifesto-july-2016/. Last accessed: 3 May 2019.

Bandura, A. (1977). Self-efficacy: Toward a Unifying Theory of Behavioral Change. In *Psychological Review* 84(2), 191–215.

Bandura, A. Ross, D., & Ross, S. A. (1963). Imitation of Film–Mediated Aggressive Models. In *Journal of Abnormal and Social Psychology* 66(1), 3–11.

Barbrook, R., & Cameron, A. (1995). *The Californian Ideology*. URL: https://www.metamute.org/editorial/articles/californian-ideology. Last accessed: 14 October 2017.

Barlow, J. P. (1996). *A Declaration of the Independence of Cyberspace*. URL: https://www.eff.org/de/cyberspace-independence. Last accessed: 23 August 2017.

Barthes, R. (2008). The Death of the Author. In D. Lodge & N. Woog (Eds.), *Modern Criticism and Theory: A Reader* (pp. 313–316). London: Routledge.

Baudrillard, J. (1986). *Requiem for the Media*. URL: http://shmacek.faculty. noctrl. edu/Courses/MediaCritSyllabusSPR2_files/19-baudrillard-03.pdf. Last accessed: 3 May 2017.

Baumeister, B., & Negator, Z. (2007). *Situationistische Revolutionstheorie. Eine Aneignung*. Stuttgart: Schmetterling.

Berner-Lee, T., Cailliau, R., Luotonen, A., Nielsen, H. F., & Secret, A. (1994). *The World Wide Web*. URL: http://storm.usc.edu/~Black/IML-400/fall-2012/readings/berners-lee_et_al_ the_world-wide_web.pdf. Last accessed: 14 October 2017.

Biebricher, T. (2012). *Neoliberalismus zur Einführung*. Hamburg: Junius.

Brandt, D. (2009). Postmoderne Wissensorganisation oder: Wie subversiv ist Wikipedia? In *Liberas. Library Ideas* 14, 4–18.

Boltanski, L., & Chiapello, È. (1999). *The New Spirit of Capitalism*. London: Verso.

Bösch, F. (2019). *Mediengeschichte*. Frankfurt am Main: Suhrkamp.

Bourdieu, P. (2001). *Masculine Domination*. Stanford, CA: Stanford University Press.

Bröckling, U. (2015). The *Entrepreneurial Self. Fabricating a New Type of Subject*. Thousand Oaks, CA: Sage.

Bruner, J. S. (2009). *The Process of Education, Revised Edition*. Cambridge, MA: Harvard University Press.

Bubner, R. (2004). Einleitung. In R. Bubner (Ed.), *Geschichte der Philosophie in Text und Darstellung. Deutscher Idealismus* (pp. 7–28). Stuttgart: Reclam.

Buchanan, M. (2011). *Privacy and Power in Social Space: Facebook*. Stirling: University of Stirling: URL: https://dspace.stir.ac.uk/bitstream/1893/9150/1/PhD%20 thesis%20.docx

Bürger, P. (1996). *Der französische Surrealismus. Studien zur avantgardistischen Literatur*. Frankfurt am Main: Suhrkamp.

Bush, V. (1945). As We May Think. In *The Atlantic Monthly* July 1945, 112–124.

Careerbuilder.com (2012) *Thirty-Seven Percent of Companies Use Social Networks to Research Potential Job Candidates*. URL: http://www.careerbuilder.com/share/ aboutus/pressreleasesdetail.aspx?id=pr691&sd=4/18/2012&ed=4/18/2099&sitei d=cbpr&sc_mp1=cb_pr691_. Last accessed: 14 October 2017.

Chatfield, T. (2013). *Digitale Kultur. 50 Schlüsselideen*. Heidelberg: Springer.

Chen, G. M. (2007). Media (Literacy) Education in the United States. In *China Media Research* 3 (2007) 3, 87–103.

Chiang, J. K. H., & Suen, H. Y. (2015). Self-Presentation and Hiring Recommendations in Online Communities: Lessons from Linked. In *Computers in Human Behavior* 48, 516–524.

Dalsgaard, C. (2005). Pedagogical Quality in e-Learning. In *Eleed* 1(1). URL: https://eleed.campussource.de/archive/1/78. Last accessed: 30.5.2015.

Deleuze, G. (2004). *Desert Islands: and Other Texts*. Los Angeles, CA: Semiotext(e).

Desrosières, A. (2005). *Die Politik der großen Zahlen. Eine Geschichte der statistischen Denkweise*. Wiesbaden: VS Springer.

Dommann, M. (2008). Papierstau und Informationsfluss. Die Normierung der Bibliothekskopie. In *Historische Anthropologie* 16(1), 31–54.

Döring, N. (2017). Internet. In B. Schorb, A. Hartung-Griemberg & C. Dallmann (Eds.), *Grundbegriffe Medienpädagogik* (pp. 163–173). München: Kopaed.

Downes, S. (2005). E-Learning 2.0. e-Learn-Magazine, URL: www.elearnmag. org/sub-page.cfm?section=articles&article=29-1. Last accessed: 01 June 2017.

Durkheim, E. (1972). *Erziehung und Soziologie*. Düsseldorf: Schwann.

Ehlers, U. D. (2011). *Qualität im E-Learning aus Lernersicht*. Wiesbaden: VS Springer.

Eisenstein, E. L. (2005). *The Printing Revolution in Early Modern Europe*. Cambridge, MA: Cambridge University Press.

Elschenbroich, D. (2000). Das Kind als Modell. Das heillose Jahrhundert vergöttert ein Bild erlöster Kindheit und endet mit einem Zögern. In M. Jeismann (Ed.), *Das 20. Jahrhundert. Welt der Extreme* (pp. 41–46). München: Beck.

Faucher, K. (2013). Thumbstruck: The Semiotics of Liking via the "Phaticon". *Semiotic Review* Nr. 3. URL: http://www.semioticreview.com/pdf/open2013/faucher_semioticsofliking.pdf. Last accessed: 23 September 2017.

Faulstich, W. (2004). *Medienwissenschaft*. Paderborn: Fink.

Feierabend, S., Plankenhorn, T., & Rathgeb, T. (2014). *JIM 2014 Jugend, Information, (Multi-) Media. Basisstudie zum Medienumgang*. URL: http://www.sainetz.at/dokumente/JIM-Studie_2014.pdf. Lase accessed: 26 July 2017.

Fleischer, S., & Hajok, D. (2016). *Einführung in die medienpädagogische Praxis und Forschung. Kinder und Jugendliche im Spannungsfeld der Medien*. Weinheim: Beltz/Juventa.

Foucault, M. (2008). *The Birth of Biopolitics. Lectures at the Collège de France, 1978–97*. Hampshire: Palgrave.

Fraser, N. (1992). Rethinking the Public Sphere: A Contribution to the Critique of Actually Existing Democracy. In C. Calhoun (Ed.), *Habermas and the Public Sphere* (S. 109–142). Cambridge, MA: MIT Press.

Freinet, C. (1990). *Cooperative Learning and Social Change*. Toronto: Oise.

Fuhr, Laros & Taylor (2017) Transformative Learning Meets Bildung: Introduction. In A. Fuhr, T. Laros & E. Taylor (Eds.), *Transformative Learning Meets Bildung. An International Exchange Wiesbaden* (pp. ix–xvi). Rotterdam: Sense.

Gaiser, B. (2008). *Lehre im Web 2.0- Didaktisches Flickwerk oder Triumph der Individualität?* URL: http://www.e-teaching.org/didaktik/kommunika-tion/08-09-12_Gaiser_Web_ 2.0.pdf. Last accessed: 05 September 2017.

Gerber, J. (2018). *Karl Marx in Paris. Die Entdeckung des Kommunismus*. München: Piper.

Gibson, E. J. (1998). Exploratory Behavior in the Development of Perceiving, Acting, and the Acquiring of Knowledge. In *Annual Review of Psychology* 39(42), 417–430.

Gramsci, A. (1982). *Selections from the Prison Books*. London: Lawrence and Wishart.

Grafe, S. (2011). «media literacy» und «media (literacy) education» in den USA–ein Brückenschlag über den Atlantik. In *MedienPädagogik: Zeitschrift für Theorie und Praxis der Medienbildung* 20, 59–80.

Habermas, J., Lennox, S., & Lennox, F. (1964) The Public Sphere: An Encyclopedia Article. In *New German Critique*, 3, 49–55.

Han, B. C. (2013). *Im Schwarm. Ansichten des Digitalen*. Berlin: Matthes & Seitz.

Hanna, N. T. (2008). *The Justifiability of Punishment*. URL: https://surface.syr.edu/phi_etd/5. Last accessed: 26 June 2019.

Hansen, K. P. (1989). *Die Geschichte der Emotionalität*. URL: https://www.zpid.de/pub/psychologie-und-geschichte/0935-0179.1989.1_2_37-48.pdf. Last accessed: 26 June 2019.

Hartmann, F. (2006). *Globale Medienkultur. Technik, Geschichte, Theorien*. Wien: Wuv.

Herder, J. G. (2004). *Another Philosophy of History and Selected Political Writings*. Indianapolis, IN and Cambridge, MA: Hackett Publishing Company.

Hok-chun, Koo (2002). Quality Education through a Post-Modern Curriculum. In *Hong Kong Teacher's Centre Journal* 1, 56–73.

Holze, J. (2017). Das umkämpfte Wissen. Untersuchungen zu Aushandlungsprozessen in Wikipedia. In R. Biermann & D. Verständig (Hrsg), *Das umkämpfte Netz. Macht- und medienbildungstheoretische Analysen zum Digitalen* (S. 95–110). Wiesbaden: VS Springer.

Horkheimer, M. & Adorno, T.W. (2002). *Dialectic of Enlightenment*. Stanford, CA: Stanford University Press.

Horlacher, R. (2011). *Bildung*. Bern: Haupt.

Hörisch, J. (2004). *Eine Geschichte der Medien. Vom Urknall zum Internet*. Frankfurt am Main: Suhrkamp.

Humboldt, W. v. (2000). Theory on Bildung. In I. Westbury, S. Hopmann & K. Riquarts (Eds.), *Teaching as a Reflective Practice: The German Didaktik Tradition* (pp. 57–62). Mahwah, NJ: J. Erlbaum.

Hüther, J. (2017). Medienpädagogik in der Vorkriegszeit. In F. v. Gross, U. Sander & D. M. Meister (Eds.), *Die Geschichte der Medienpädagogik in Deutschland* (pp. 11–33). Weinheim: Beltz/Juventa.

Hüther, J., & Podehl, B (2017). Geschichte der Medienpädagogik. In B. Schorb, A. Hartung-Griemberg, & C. Dallmann (Eds.), *Grundbegriffe Medienpädagogik* (pp. 117–124). München: Kopaed.

Iske, S. (2015). Medienbildung. In F. v. Gross, D. M. Meister & U. Sander (Eds.), *Medienpädagogik – ein Überblick* (pp. 247–272). Weinheim: Beltz/Juventa.

Jessop, B. (1992). *Fordism and Post-Fordism: A Critical Reformulation Bob Jessop*. Preprint of Article in Pathways to Regionalism and Industrial Development. Preprint. A.J. Scott & M. J. Storper, 43–65. London: Routledge. URL: https://www.researchgate.net/publication/312017322_Fordism_and_Post-Fordism_a_Critical_Reformulation. Last accessed: 18 April 2020.

Jordan, P., & Hernandez-Reif, M. (2009). Reexamination of Young Children's Racial Attitudes and Skin Tone Preferences. In *Journal of Black Psychology* 35(3), 388–403.

Jullien, F. (2017). *Es gibt keine kulturelle Identität*. Frankfurt am Main: Suhrkamp.

Kaerlein, T. (2018). *Smartphones als digitale Nahkörpertechnologien. Zur Kybernetisierung des Alltags*. Bielefeld: Transcript.

Kammerl, R. (2017). Das Potential der Medien für die Bildung des Subjekts. Überlegungen zur Kritik der Subjektorientierung in der medienpädagogischen Theoriebildung. *MedienPädagogik* 27, 30–49. doi: 10.21240/mpaed/27/2017.01.14.X.

Kant, I. (1900) *On Education*. Boston, MA: Heath.

Kbb. (2018) *Studie Marken-Kinder 2018: Bedeutung von Marken für Kinder und Familien*. URL: https://www.kbundb.de/blog/studie-marken-kinder-2018-die-bedeutung-von-marken-fur-kinder-wird-von-markenartiklern-immer-noch-unterschatzt. Last accessed: 21 April 2019.

Kergel, D. (2011). *Subjektorientierte Sozialisationstheorie- und Praxis*. Aalborg: Institute for Learning and Philosophy, Aalborg University.

Kergel, D. (2013). *Rebellisch aus erkenntnistheoretischem Prinzip. Möglichkeiten und Grenzen angewandter Erkenntnistheorie*. Frankfurt am Main: Peter Lang.

Kergel, D. (2018). *Qualitative Bildungsforschung. Ein integrativer Ansatz.* Wiesbaden: VS Springer.

Kergel, D. (2019). *Erziehungskonstellationen analysieren und Bildungsräume gestalten. Ein Methodenbuch für die gesellschaftliche Praxis.* Wiesbaden: VS Springer.

Kergel, D. (2020). *Gedurckt – Gefunkt – Gepostet. Medienwandel und Medienpädagogik bürgerlicher Gesellschaft,* Wiesbaden: VS Springer.

Kergel, D., & Heidkamp, B. (2015). *Forschendes Lernen mit digitalen Medien – ein Lehrbuch. #theorie #praxis #evaluation.* Münster: Waxmann.

Kirpal, A., & Vogel, A. (2006). Neue Medien in einer vernetzten Gesellschaft: Zur Geschichte des Internets und des World Wide Web. In *NTM Zeitschrift für Geschichte der Wissenschaften, Technik und Medizin* 14(3), 137–147.

Kommer, S. (2017). Werbung. In B. Schorb, A. Hartung-Griemberg & C. Dallmann (Eds.), *Grundbegriffe Medienpädagogik* (pp. 401–409). München: Kopaed.

Koselleck, R. (2000). Hinter der tödlichen Linie. Das Zeitalter des Totalen. In M. Jeismann (Ed.), *Das 20. Jahrhundert. Welt der Extreme* (pp. 9–29). München: Beck.

Koselleck, R. (2002). *The Practice of Conceptual History. Timing History, Spacing Concepts.* Stanford, CA: Stanford University Press.

Koselleck, R. (2006). *Begriffsgeschichten. Studien zur Semantik und Pragmatik der politischen und sozialen Sprache.* Frankfurt am Main: Suhrkamp.

Krämer-Badoni, T. (1978). *Zur Legitimität der bürgerlichen Gesellschaft. Eine Untersuchung des Arbeitsbegriffs in den Theorien von Locke, Smith, Ricardo, Hegel und Marx.* Frankfurt am Main: Campus.

Kühn, M. (2012) *Johann Gottlieb Fichte – ein Deutscher Philosoph.* München: Beck

Lagaay, A., & Lauer, D. (2004). *Medientheorien. Eine philosophische Einführung.* Frankfurt am Main: Campus.

Lauer, G. (2017). Nachwort. In *W. v. Humboldt, Schriften zur Bildung* (S. 236–271). Stuttgart: Reclam.

Lehr, C. (2012). *Web 2.0 in der universitären Lehre. Ein Handlungsrahmen für die Gestaltung technologiegestützter Lernszenarien.* Boizenburg: Vwh.

Lessig, L. (2001). *The Future of Ideas. The Fate of the Commons in a Connected World. Creative Commons Version.* New York: Random House.

Lessig, L. (2009). *Remix, Making Art and Culture Thrive in the Hybrid Economy.* London: Bloomsbury Academic.

Ludwig, R. (2009). *Hegel für Anfänger. Phänomenologie des Geistes.* München: Dtv.

Lukács, G. (1971). *Die Theorie des Romans. Ein gesichtsphilosophischer Versuch über die Formen der großen Epik.* Neuwied: Luchterhand.

Lyotard, J. F. (1983). *The Postmodern Condition: A Report on Knowledge.* Manchester: Manchester University Press.

Mahmud, T. (2015). *Precarious Existence and Capitalism: A Permanent State of Exception.* URL: http://www.swlaw.edu/pdfs/lr/44_3mahmud. Last accessed: 22 February 2017.

Martens, H. (2010). Evaluating Media Literacy Education: Concepts, Theories and Future Directions. In *Journal of Media Literacy Education* 2 (2010) 1, 1–22.

Martensen, M., Börgmann, K., & Bick, M. (2011). The Impact of Social Networking Sites on the Employer-Employee Relationship. In *Proceedings of BLED Conference 2011.* URL: http://aisel.aisnet.org/bled2011/54/. Last accessed: 23 September 2017.

Mattig, R. (2019). *Wilhelm von Humboldt als Ethnograph: Bildungsforschung im Zeitalter der Aufklärung.* Weinheim: Beltz/Juventa.

McLuhan, M. (1964). *Understanding Media.* New York: Mentor.

McLuhan. M. (2011). *The Gutenberg Galaxy. The Making of the Typographic Man.* Toronto: University of Toronto Press.

Mersch, D. (2006). *Medientheorien zur Einführung.* Hamburg: Junius.

Mikos, L. (2018). Fernsehen. In D. Hoffmann & R. Winter (Eds.), *Mediensoziologie. Handbuch für Wissenschaft und Studium* (pp. 195–201). Baden-Baden: Nomos.

Mitrou, L., Kandias, M., Stavrou, V., & Gritzalis, D. (2014). *Social Media Profiling: A Panopticon or omnipoticon tool?* URL: https://www.infosec.aueb.gr/Publications/2014-SSN-Privacy%20Social%20Media.pdf. Last accessed: 23 September 2017.

Müller-Dohm, S. (2018). Medientheorie und Öffentlichkeitsforschung. In D. Hoffmann & R. Winkler (Eds.), *Mediensoziologie. Handbuch für Wissenschaft und Studium* (pp. 146–157). Baden-Baden: Nomos.

Musloff, H.-U. (1989). *Bildung. Der klassische Begriff und sein Wandel in der Bildungsreform der sechziger Jahre.* Weinheim: Deutscher Studien Verlag.

Nadkarni, A., & Hofmann, S. G. (2012). Why Do People Use Facebook? In *Personality and Individual Differences* 52(3), 243–249.

Nelson, T. H. (1965). Complex Information Processing: A File Structure for the Complex, the Changing and the Indeterminate. In *Proceedings of the 1965 20th National Conference* (pp. 84–100). New York: ACM.

Niedermair, K. (1992). Das Ideal der philosophischen Postmoderne: Widerstand gegen die Okkupationen des Ideals in der Moderne. In A. Hütter, T. Hug, J. Perger (Eds.), *Paradigmenvielfalt und Wissensintegration. Beiträge zur Postmoderne im Umkreis von Jean-Francois Lyotard* (pp. 87–98). Wien: Passagen.

Noble, S. (2018). *Algorithms of Oppression: How Search Engines Reinforce Racism.* New York: New York University Press.

Oelkers, J. (1995) Reformpädagogik: Aktualität und Historie. In W. Böhm & J. Oelkers (Eds.), *Reformpädagogik kontrovers* (pp. 23–47). Würzburg: Ergon.

O'Reilly, T. (2006). Web 2.0 Compact Definition: Trying Again. URL: http://radar.oreilly.com/archives/2006/12/web-20-compact.html. Last accessed: 18 May 2019.

Payer, P. (2017). Geräusche und Lärm der Großstadt um 1900. In G. Paul & R. Schock (Eds.), *Sound des Jahrhunderts* (pp. 36–41). Bonn: Bpb.

Peitz, M., & Schwalbe, U. (2016). *Zwischen Sozialromantik und Neoliberalismus – zur Ökonomie der Sharing-Economy* (No. 16–033). ZEW Discussion Papers.

Postman, N. (2000). The Humanism of Media Ecology. In *Proceedings of the Media Ecology Association*, Nr. 1, 10–16. URL: https://www.media-ecology.org/resources/Documents/Proceedings/v1/v1-02-Postman.pdf. Last accessed: 25 July 2019.

Prensky, M. (2001). Digital Natives, Digital Immigrants. In *On The Horizon* 9 (5). URL: http://www.marcprensky.com/writing/Prensky%20-%20Digital%20Natives,%20Digital%20Immigrants%20-%20Part1.pdf. Last accessed: 6 January 2019.

Prokop, D. (1974). *Massenkultur und Spontanität. Zur veränderten Warenform der Massenkommunikation im Spätkapitalismus.* Frankfurt am Main: Suhrkamp.

Prokop, D. (2001). *Der Kamp um die Medien. Das Geschichtsbuch der neuen kritischen Medienforschung.* Hamburg: Vsa.

Prokop, D. (2004). *Gegen Medien-Lügen. Das neue Lexikon der Kulturindustrie.* Hamburg: Vsa.

Ravenscroft, A. (2011). Dialogue and Connectivism: A New Approach to Understanding and Promoting Dialogue-rich Networked Learning. In *The International Review of Research in Open and Distributed Learning* 12(3), 139–160.

Reckwitz, A. (2003). Grundelemente einer Theorie sozialer Praktiken. Eine sozialtheoretische Perspektive. In *Zeitschrift für Soziologie* 32(4), 282–301.

Reckwitz, S. (2012). *Das hybride Subjekt. Eine Theorie der Subjekkulturen von der bürgerlichen Moderne zur Postmoderne.* Weilerswirst: Velbrück.

Reich, K. (2012). *Konstruktivistische Didaktik: Das Lehr- und Studienbuch mit Online-Methodenpool.* Weinheim: Beltz/Juventa.

Resch, C., & Steiner, H. (2016). *Kapitalismus.* Münster: Westfälisches Dampfboot.

Reichardt, R. (2008). Plurimediale Kommunikation und symbolische Repräsentation in den Französischen Revolutionen 1789–1848. In S. Grampp et al. (Eds.) *Revolutionsmedien – Medienrevolutionen* (pp. 231–275). Konstanz: Uvk.

Ricken, N. (2006). *Die Ordnung der Bildung. Beiträge zu einer Genealogie der Bildung.* Wiesbaden: VS Springer.

Şahin, M. (2012). Pros and Cons of Connectivism as a Learning Theory. *International Journal of Physical and Social Sciences* 2(4), 437–454.

Schmitz, S., & Daniels, A. (2006). *Die Geschichte des Kapitalismus. Vom Wohlstand zum World Wide Web.* München: Heyne.

Schelhowe, H. (2007). *Technologie, Imagination und Lernen: Grundlagen für Bildungsprozesse mit Digitalen Medien.* Münster: Waxmann.

Schivelbusch, W. (1990). *Das Paradies, der Geschmack und die Vernunft.* Frankfurt am Main: Fischer.

Schmidt, E., & Cohen, J. (2013). *The New Digital Age. Reshaping the Future of People, Nations and Business.* London: John Murray.

Schweppenhäuser, G. (1996). *Theodor W. Adorno. Zur Einführung.* Hamburg: Junius.

Seel, N. (1999). Instruktionsdesign: Modelle und Anwendungsgebiete. In *Unterrichtswissenschaft* 27, 2–11.

Sharples, M., Taylor, J. & Vavoula, G. (2005). Towards a Theory of Mobile Learning. In *Proceedings of mLearn* 1(1), 1–9.

Siemens, G. (2004). Connectivism: A Learning Theory for the Digital Age. In *International Journal of Instructional Technology and Distance Learning* 2(1), 3–10.

Simmel, G. (1969). The Metropolis and the Mental Life. In R. Sennet (Ed.). *Classic Essays in the Culture of Cities* (pp. 47–60). Upper Saddle River, NJ: Prentice Hall.

Skinner, B. F. (2011). *About Behaviorism.* London: Random House.

Spivak, C. G. (2008). *Can the Subaltern Speak?* Cambridge, MA: Harvard University Press.

Springer, S., Birch, K., & MacLeavy, J. (2016). An Introduction to Neoliberalism. In S. Springer, K. Birch & J. MacLeavy (Eds.), *The Handbook of Neoliberalism* (pp. 1–14). New York: Routledge.

Srnicek, N. (2017). *Plattform-Kapitalismus.* Hamburg: His.

Stalder, F. (2016). *Kultur der Digitalität.* Frankfurt am Main: Suhrkamp.

Standage, T. (2006). *Das viktorianische Internet. Die erstaunliche Geschichte des Telegraphen und der Online-Pioniere des 19. Jahrhunderts.* St Gallen: Midas.

The Mentor (2004). *The Hacker Manifesto. The Conscience of a Hacker.* URL: http://www. it-academy.cc/article/1375/Das+Manifest+von+The+Mentor.html. Last accessed: 1 September 2017.

Turkle, S. (2011). *Life on the Screen: Identity in the Age of the Internet.* New York: Simon & Schuster.

Tyner, K. (2007): Media Literacy, Aims and Purposes of. In J. J. Arnett (Ed.), *Encyclopedia of Children, Adolescents, and the Media* (pp. 523–525). London: Sage.

Vogel, M. (2013). 1968 als Kommunikationsereignis. Die Rolle des Fernsehens. In I. Gilcher-Holtey (Ed.), *Horizont-Verschiebungen des Politischen in den 1960er und 1970er Jahren* (pp. 47–82). München: Oldenbourg.

Weel, A. v. d. (2011). *Changing our Textual Minds. Towards a Digital Order of Knowledge.* Manchester: Manchester University Press.

Wegener, C. (2017). Fernsehen. In B. Schorb, A. Hartung-Griemberg & C. Dallmann (Eds.), *Grundbegriffe der Medienpädagogik* (pp. 90–93). München: Kopaed.

Wheeler, S. (2008). *All Changing: The Social Web and the Future of Higher Education.* URL: http://www.slid/timbuckteeth/all-changing-t-he-social-web-and-the-future-of-higher-education-presentation. Last accessed: 8 August 2018.

Wiedemann, C. (2018). *Kritische Kollektivität im Netz. Anonymous, Facebook und die Kraft der Affizierung in der Kontrollgesellschaft.* Bielefeld: Transcript.

Willey, L., White, B. J., Domagalski, T., & Ford, J. C. (2012). Candidate-screening, Information Technology and the Law: Social Media Considerations. In *Issues in Information Systems* 13(1), 300–309.

Wimmer, J. (2018). Partizipation und Gegen-Öffentlichkeit. In D. Hoffmann & R. Winkler (Eds.), *Mediensoziologie, Handbuch für Wissenschaft und Studium* (pp. 247–254). Baden-Baden: Nomos.

Winkel, S., Petermann, F., & Petermann U. (2006). *Lernpsychologie.* Paderborn: Schöningh.

Yaakoby, T. (2012). *A Critical Examination of NeoMarxist and Postmodernist Theories as Applied to Education.* Münster: Waxmann.

Yeh, S. (2013). *Anything Goes? Postmodern Medientheorien im Vergleich. Die großen (Medien-)Erzählungen von McLuhan, Baudrillard, Virilio, Kittler und Flusser.* Bielefeld: Transcript.

Zorn, I. (2011). Medienkompetenz und Medienbildung mit Fokus auf Digitale Medien. In: H. Moser, P. Grell & H. Niesyto (Eds.), *Medienbildung und Medienkompetenz. Beiträge zu Schlüsselbegriffen der Medienpädagogik* (pp. 211–235). München: kopead.

Index

Note: *Italic* page numbers refer to figures and page numbers followed by "n" denote endnotes.

Printed in the United States
By Bookmasters